This book helps us focus clearly on the death and resurrection of the Lord Jesus, which is a commendation in itself. It does so by engaging with the Bible, exploring passages from Old and New Testaments in a fresh and lively way, and all with deep practical challenges to daily life. I particularly liked the challenges to corporate Christian life alongside the personal challenges. It was also great to see the neglected subjects of baptism and communion given their proper place.

Full of profound quotes and gripping stories, this is a book to enjoy and discuss, but most of all to renew our joy and fire up a passion for discipleship.

Andy Bathgate, Chief Executive, Scripture Union, Scotland

This work is certainly worth being included among the recent tomes on the cross. The authors add their voice with clarity, scholarship and practical wisdom for those wanting to reflect on the significance and implications of Jesus' death and resurrection for us today. It is a demonstration of putting theory into practice in an accessible manner. If you read it alone or use it with a group, you will be reminded of and impacted by the power of the amazing cross.

Dotha Blackwood, Tutor in Practical Theology, Spurgeon's College, London

At the cross we see most clearly the loving heart of our God. Jeremy and Elizabeth McQuoid help us glimpse something of that love and of how we now stand before such a glorious God. And, from these heart-stopping truths, how irresistibly the cross draws from us praise, love and changed lives in response.

Mark Ellis, Team Leader, UCCF Scotland

A delightfully clear and tender account of Jesus' work on the cross. Fully aware of the challenges to the historic Christian faith on the significance of Christ's work for us, the McQuoids have powerfully explained and applied the teaching of the cross for today. And in Keswick tradition they have driven that message home to our hearts as well as our minds, showing us how the cross defines the Christian's life in the world, and leaving us worshipping at the feet of the Lamb of God.

Liam Goligher, Senior Minister, Tenth Presbyterian Church Philadelphia, USA

Skilfully blends clear Bible teaching, practical application and effective illustration. I especially appreciate the passion and conviction which have shaped this book. It is an ideal introduction to the heart of the Christian gospel, and a very welcome addition to the Keswick Foundation series.
Jonathan Lamb, Chairman, Keswick Ministries

In days of confusion surrounding the doctrine of the atonement, I have been looking for a book which is clear on the doctrine, but also conveys the sheer wonder of the truth of Christ dying in our place, and the implications for our lives. This is the book I have been waiting for!
Peter Maiden, International Coordinator for Operation Mobilization and former chairman of the Keswick Convention

Jeremy and Liz McQuoid have written a book that is so simply, clearly and interestingly presented that it will make the message of the cross of Jesus come home vividly to you. But this is not a book for passive 'dummies' who simply want to read an interesting story; it is for people who are willing to be open to the obligation that the death of Jesus places upon them to make their own personal commitment to him as their Saviour and Lord.
I. Howard Marshall, Professor Emeritus of New Testament, University of Aberdeen

The key to spiritual vitality in the Christian life is to stay close to the cross of Christ. With freshness and clarity the authors write about the things of first importance in a way that causes praise and life-changing worship.
Paul Rees, Senior Pastor, Charlotte Chapel, Edinburgh

No matter where we are in our Christian experience we live in sight of the cross. We can never get over it or fully understand love 'so amazing, so divine'. Here is a book that has something for everyone who lives within the shadow of Jesus Christ and him crucified.
Haddon Robinson, Harold John Ockenga Distinguished Professor of Preaching at Gordon-Conwell Theological Seminary, Boston

What more could one ask than to have the significance of the momentous events of the death and resurrection of the Lord Jesus explained and applied clearly, passionately and faithfully? This book does just that and it will encourage all who read it to delight in Christ Jesus, marvel at his magnificent work, and live grateful gospel-centred lives.

Alan J. Thompson, Lecturer in New Testament at Sydney Missionary and Bible College, Australia, and author of The Acts of the Risen Lord Jesus *(IVP)*

THE
AMAZING
CROSS

JEREMY & ELIZABETH McQUOID

ivp

THE AMAZING CROSS

Transforming lives today

INTER-VARSITY PRESS
Norton Street, Nottingham NG7 3HR, England
Email: ivp@ivpbooks.com
Website: www.ivpbooks.com

First published 2012

British Library Cataloguing in Publication Data
A catalogue record for this book is available from the British Library.

ISBN: 978–1–84474–587–1

Set in Dante 12/15pt
Typeset in Great Britain by CRB Associates, Potterhanworth, Lincolnshire
Printed in Great Britain by Ashford Colour Press Ltd, Gosport, Hampshire

Inter-Varsity Press publishes Christian books that are true to the Bible and that communicate the gospel, develop discipleship and strengthen the church for its mission in the world.

Inter-Varsity Press is closely linked with the Universities and Colleges Christian Fellowship, a student movement connecting Christian Unions in universities and colleges throughout Great Britain, and a member movement of the International Fellowship of Evangelical Students. Website: www.uccf.org.uk

To Mark, Daniel and Nathan –
Praying that you will grow to be men of the cross

Contents

Foreword

For over 130 years, the Keswick Convention has played a vital role in bringing high-quality Bible teaching and spiritual renewal to the evangelical community. As a result, many thousands of people who have attended the convention have been blessed. The vision of this exciting family of books is to share that blessing with the many other people who may know and honour the name of Keswick, but who have little understanding of the convention's core values and commitments.

The titles aim to provide key studies into many of the themes and emphases which have characterized and shaped the convention over the years. Our prayer is that, as a result, a new generation will be inspired again, in the words of our motto text, to be 'All One in Christ Jesus', and to participate in his mission in the world.

Husband and wife authors, Jeremy and Elizabeth McQuoid, have done a marvellous job in helping us understand the centrality of the cross in Keswick's history and teaching, reminding us of the awesome wonder of God's love and grace in bringing us salvation through giving us his Son as the sacrifice for our sins. May you be encouraged and strengthened with confidence in the gospel as you read this book, and inspired to take up your cross and follow our crucified Lord.

John Risbridger, Chairman, Keswick Council

Acknowledgments

We are grateful to the Keswick Convention trustees for inviting us to write this book. It has been a privilege to wrestle with such a tremendous theme. We have enjoyed working together as a husband-and-wife team, but will leave you to guess which chapters each of us wrote!

Sincere thanks are due to those who provided us with helpful insights: Jonathan Lamb, Peter Maiden, Steve Brady, and especially Georgina Smallman and Matt Sleeman, whose copious notes on our manuscript made us feel that 'no stone had been left unturned'.

We are also thankful to Eleanor Trotter, IVP's Senior Commissioning Editor, for her attention to detail and warm encouragements. And above all we thank the Lord, not just for his help in bringing the book together, but most especially for the cross itself. While we hope this book will help you draw closer to Christ, we are also keenly aware that no words can ultimately do justice to 'Christ crucified'.

Our prayer is that the Holy Spirit will use the thoughts in this book to direct you to deeper places than words can reach and help you wonder once again at the cross of Christ.

Introduction: Keswick and the cross

So what is the secret of Keswick's success? The convention's 135-year history makes it quite simply the longest-running Bible teaching event anywhere in the world, which is a significant achievement amid the constantly-changing trends and fashions of our day.

When I (Jeremy) was a divinity student in Chicago ten years ago, I remember hearing about 'Keswick theology' in a systematic theology class. Clearly the impact of Keswick has been worldwide, and it is more than an annual convention. In many ways it is a movement that has impacted evangelical Christianity around the globe.

What began in 1875 with a single week of teaching from some of the world's most gifted Bible teachers, has now been transformed into three packed-out weeks, where around 12,000 people, from all different backgrounds, creeds and ages, squeeze into this enchanting town in the heart of the Lake District, to worship, to talk mission and, most especially, to hear from God's word.

Enduring truth

So what is Keswick's secret? We could probably mention several things, and no doubt the sheer beauty of the surrounding Cumbrian mountains kissing picturesque lakes adds to the allure. If you were to add up in Scripture all the times God's people met with him in a tent, or by a lake, or up a mountain, you will realize that Keswick offers unique opportunities to meet with the Lord!

But first and foremost I think Keswick has stood the test of time because of its commitment to enduring truth. This book is part of the Keswick Foundations series, which seeks to express, in plain twenty-first-century language, the central themes that have driven Keswick throughout its history. And one of those themes, dare we say the major theme, is the cross of Christ.

In preparation for writing this book, we have browsed through some of the great preaching that has graced the Keswick platform down the years, and it has struck us how central the proclamation of the cross has been throughout Keswick's lifetime. For many years in the early part of the twentieth century, every Tuesday night was devoted to the meaning and application of the cross.

You will find quotes from past Keswick sermons liberally strewn throughout this book, and recognize almost a 'Who's Who' of evangelical preachers – from Donald Grey Barnhouse and G. B. Duncan, through to John Stott and Alec Motyer, to Steve Gaukroger and Alistair Begg – preachers past and present who chose 'to know nothing except Christ and him crucified'.

Oberammergau

The cross of Christ has a magnetic appeal of course, not just in Keswick, but around the world, and not just now, but forever. That fact came home to me (Jeremy) forcibly in 2010 when several friends from my church in Aberdeen told me they were going to Oberammergau. I had never heard the name Oberammergau before, so I was intrigued enough to make some investigations.

Oberammergau is a very out-of-the-way little German village. Why did so many Scots want to board a plane to get to such an obscure setting in the Bavarian outback? What was it about this village that gave it such pulling power?

The answer lies in a passion play that these German villagers perform once every ten years. The history behind the play is dramatic in itself. Back in 1632 this little village was suffering under the ravages of the bubonic plague. Conditions grew so desperate that twenty people died in the month of March 1633 alone.

And so the residents of the town got together in crisis mode and made an amazing vow to God, that if God spared their town from the effects of the plague, they would put on a play every ten years for the rest of time, depicting the death of Christ.

After the townsfolk made that decision, the effects of the plague began to wane. By July 1633, the death rate had fallen to just one. The play was first performed in 1634. These very ordinary German villagers were convinced that God had indeed spared them.

From those small beginnings, this passion play has now become a worldwide phenomenon. It has been performed by successive generations of villagers over the last four hundred years, during the first year of every new decade, most recently in 2010, when 102 performances were held between 15 May and 3 October.

On *Wikipedia* you will find a famous photograph of the American entrepreneur Henry Ford (of the Ford car company) attending the play back in 1930, and a very old grainy photo of 'Jesus' and 'the Apostle John' from the 1900 performance. The play has so captured the imagination that over 2,000 performers, musicians and stage technicians are involved – all of them residents of the village. The stage itself is built on the very graveyard where many of the victims of the plague were buried, so that the play's unique 'vow-to-God' history would be remembered.

Around 500,000 people jet in from around the world to witness the play. But the performance itself is not for the faint hearted. It lasts seven hours, from 2:30 in the afternoon until 10:30 at night, with a three-hour supper interval. The play starts with Jesus entering Jerusalem, continues through his death on the cross and finishes with the resurrection.

While the actors are speaking and singing their way through the passion events, a series of tapestries is displayed in the background, depicting some of the rich Old Testament symbolism that points to the cross, such as images of the sacrificial system from Leviticus and the bronze serpent in the wilderness.

The play has been attacked by various authorities over the years, and edits have been made to the text to remove any unnecessary anti-Jewish sentiment (which Hitler wanted to keep, back in the 1930s), but by and large the play has continued to be a faithful retelling of the epic story of the cross for almost half a millennium.

It remains a remarkable testimony to the magnetism of the cross of Christ that in our twenty-first-century post-Christian culture, half a million people will fly halfway across the world to view a seven-hour retelling of the events behind Good Friday. It is thrilling to think that a little village in Germany should have its identity so powerfully shaped by the cross, and that generation after generation have kept the promise to promote the cross of Christ as the answer to humanity's deepest need.

The magnetism of the cross

And it is this magnetism behind the cross that has encouraged us to write this book. Our aim is not to write a complex theological tome that looks good on the shelf, but never gets opened. What we hope to achieve is to bring the message of the cross through your front door on a Monday morning.

On the one hand, we want to unpack rich theological terms like propitiation, justification, reconciliation and redemption, and make them live in your heart. But on the other hand, about half this book is devoted to the practical application of the cross in our daily lives.

'How then ought we to live?' is the cry that should come from each of our hearts every time we receive a truth from Scripture. And especially when we face the theme of themes: the cross of our Lord Jesus. We hope to show that the cross is not a relic from the past that we admire from a distance, as we would admire a stained-glass window. The cross is to be lived and sung and cherished in our lives today. Its shadow needs to fall on everything we ever think and feel and do. The cross is heaven's grandest theme (Revelation 5:9–10), the source of our salvation, but it's also the motive behind our daily obedience.

A drama in four parts

Let us give you some kind of road map for this book. It is laid out in four parts.

Part one asks the question, 'What happened at the cross?' We want to start with the great theme of the love of God expressed in God sacrificing his Son. That will lead us into the difficult but vital question of God's holiness and our sin. We will consider just how God, out of sheer love, decided to pour out his righteous wrath against sin on Christ instead of us, before finally looking at the cross as the defeat of Satan.

Part two asks, 'What difference does the cross make to me?' These chapters draw together the great themes of justification, that I can be declared righteous through the cross of Christ; redemption, that I can be set free from my slavery to sin; and reconciliation, that I can have peace with God and other believers through the cross.

In part three, we want to get into the nitty-gritty of daily life, under the heading, 'How can I live a cross-shaped life?' What did Jesus mean when he said to his disciples, 'Take up your cross and follow me'? We will tackle the thorny issue of suffering, before considering the two great ordinances of the church: baptism and communion.

In the final part, we will concentrate on the resurrection, without which the cross has no power. So we will look not simply at the facts of the resurrection, but how Christ's resurrection guarantees our future resurrection, and the breathtaking thought of cosmic renewal.

If you finish this book thinking that the cross and resurrection of Christ is the most important thing that has ever happened or will ever happen, then we will have achieved our goal. The cross is our death, our life, our motive for living and our hope for the future.

May this book glorify God and lead us to Christ, by the power of the Spirit.

Part one:
What happened at the cross?

1

The passion of the cross

Nothing affects us quite as deeply as what happens to our children. That truth struck me forcibly when I recently came across this diary entry of a Christian in Texas called Tim White, whose young son had experienced great suffering in his early years.

In the first 15 years of his life, our son Ryan had over 30 surgeries. When he was about eight years old, he was in the hospital for another surgery. The medical staff had already given him the 'Barney Juice,' a purple liquid with something like morphine in it.

The medical staff then began to roll his surgical bed to the operating room. As usual, we accompanied him to the two big doors that led to the place of surgery. That is where we stopped, and told him all would be okay for the last time before surgery.

This day, as we got to the doors and they opened, he sat up in the bed, looked me in the eyes and pleaded, 'Dad, don't let them take me!'

At that moment, my heart was broken. I would have done anything to take him off that bed except for the fact he had to have the surgery. That knowledge didn't ease the pain in my heart at all. I just stood there trembling as the doors closed, and he disappeared. That is when I broke down into tears.

Shortly after, when I was asking God how such a good love could hurt so much, I realized that he had gone through the same thing. In the Garden of Gethsemane Jesus prayed: 'Father, if there is any other way, let this cup pass from me.' Translated into the language of a child, 'Daddy, don't let them take me.'

I allowed the surgeons to take my son for his own good. God allowed the crucifiers to take his Son for our good. That is how much God loves us. It has been said that *something is worth what someone else is willing to pay*. Christ's willingness to give his life shows the value he placed on me.[1]

Sometimes we fall into the trap of thinking about the cross of Christ in a detached way. We think through the logic of salvation: we are sinners, God provided the remedy, and we either accept that remedy, like a doctor's prescription, or we reject it. But that is a very cold way of looking at the cross.

It removes us from the passion that flows through the veins of God every time he thinks about the cross. The cross is about a Father 'giving' his beloved Son, in the most extraordinary, bloody, offensive, heart-wrenching, glorious sacrifice ever offered.

And if our hearts are to be captivated, if our souls are to be grabbed in the grip of the cross, we need to throw ourselves into the deeply emotional relationship that has always existed between the Father and the Son. It's like plunging into a measureless ocean.

God's emotions are stirred when he thinks of his Son. This comes through loudly and clearly when you read Mark's account of Jesus' baptism. Jesus' baptism is the moment when Christ took his first step out of Nazareth obscurity into the public limelight.

And as Jesus comes out of the river Jordan, Mark says the heavens were 'ripped open'. Mark deliberately uses a passionate, eye-catching phrase. It's the same phrase he later uses for the ripping of the temple curtain during the crucifixion. God ripped the heavens open to declare to the world, 'You are my Son, whom I love' (Mark 1:11).

The Father delights in his Son

What is striking about this ripping open of heaven is that Jesus hadn't really done anything yet to make his Father delight in him. At his baptism, Christ was around thirty years old. Apart from a brief, dramatic encounter in the temple as a twelve-year-old, where Jesus amazed the theology professors with his learning, he has lived up to this point in quiet Nazareth (and had probably already attended his human father's funeral).

He hasn't calmed a storm or exorcized a demon, fed five thousand, or preached the Sermon on the Mount. He has not achieved anything of any note in public, and yet the Father rips open the heavens to tell the world what he thinks of his darling Son.

And we suddenly enter into the mysterious inner relationship between God the Father and God the Son, the love that existed between them before the world began. God is thrilled with his Son in every way. The Son doesn't have to do anything public or dramatic to please him.

I recently went to watch my five-year-old son perform in a school play. His show-stopping performance involved walking on stage, dressed in a cardboard cut-out of a bus. It wasn't

exactly Oscar-winning material – he didn't even have any
words to say. But there I was, alongside his mother, on the
front row – we had deliberately arrived half an hour early to
get the best seats in the house. And at one stage my wife had
to encourage me to stop clicking the camera, as I was taking
so many photos of *my boy*. He did not have to do anything
special to please me. I was delighting in who he was.

Multiply my feelings by a million and you will understand
how enraptured the Father is by his darling Son. While occasionally our children may stretch our patience, the Father is
continuously delighted with the perfection and obedience of
his Son.

And so God rips open heaven, before Jesus has done
anything significant, to tell the world he delights in his Son.
Until we understand the love that exists between Father and
Son, our hearts will never really grasp what it cost the Father
to 'give' us his Son in the startling, bloody way that he did.
Divine passion flames out from the cross.

The Word became flesh

John's Gospel is the section of Scripture that delves most
deeply into the love shared between the Father and Son. The
Gospel opens, like a great West End theatre production, in
the most dramatic way. Matthew and Luke start with Jesus'
birth story, Mark goes straight to the ministry of John the
Baptist, but John pulls back the curtain of heaven to reveal
this unique relationship that existed between Father and Son
before the world began: 'in the beginning was the Word'.

John, with his phrase 'in the beginning', clearly wants us to
think back to Genesis 1. And we find that when that great
beginning began, the Word (Jesus) was already 'with' God.
Father and Son were in a permanent state of emotional,
eternal fellowship with each other. John says the Son was 'in

closest relationship with the Father' (John 1:18). And you sense the magnitude of the decision taken in heaven, when the Word 'became flesh' (John 1:14). The word is, literally, 'tabernacled': John is telling us that God's presence was as real in Jesus as it was when his glory filled the tabernacle in the middle of Israel's camp in Old Testament times.

Even at his birth, God flooded the night sky over Bethlehem with angels praising God for his unspeakable gift. If all we had was the incarnation of Jesus, that in itself would have been a dramatic 'giving' of God's Son to us.

'Giving' at the cross

But moving from the Father's side to his crude Bethlehem stable was just the beginning of God 'giving' us his Son.

It was not the incarnation that was uppermost in John's mind when he later penned that great verse which encapsulates all the passion of the gospel: 'For God so loved the world that he gave his one and only Son, so that whoever believes in him should not perish but have eternal life' (John 3:16). The incarnation is no doubt part of that 'giving', but it is not Jesus coming into our world that means believers will not perish. We are only saved from judgment, and catapulted into God's eternal life, through the cross.

When this glorious, eternal Father 'gave' his beloved Son, who had been at his side in perfect loving fellowship for all eternity, he was signing Jesus' death warrant. He was picturing the day when Christ would be writhing in agony, barely recognizable as a human being, with soldier spit running down his cheeks, lifting up his crushed lungs for air, and crying out, 'My God, my God why have you forsaken me?' (Matthew 27:46; Mark 15:34).

The cross takes this 'giving' to a whole new level. The Father gave us his Son in the fullest way imaginable. And one way to grasp the real passion behind the cross, the emotions between Father and Son during those three hours of Calvary darkness, would be to go behind the scenes of a deeply emotional Old Testament story about another father who was called to sacrifice a beloved son.

Abraham and Isaac

The story of Abraham sacrificing Isaac (Genesis 22:1–19) is perhaps the most disturbing of all Old Testament narratives. Isaac was Abraham's beloved son. There must have been a particularly powerful bond between them because of the wait Abraham and Sarah went through on the bumpy journey towards Isaac's birth. We have noticed the bond that mothers have with children for whom they have waited over a long period of time, or whose incubators they have sat beside, praying for their little one in a fight for life.

Isaac was that kind of beloved son. Abraham and Sarah were childless, and beyond hope of conceiving; in their nineties when God told them they would have a 'child of the promise' the next year. Isaac was truly a son sent from heaven. So much of this story is a powerful foreshadowing of the Father-Son emotions at the cross.

But in Genesis 22:2 God comes to Abraham one day and tells him to sacrifice his 'one and only son'. The wording is so important here. The Hebrew expression is the exact phrase that John later picks up in John 3:16 to describe God giving us Jesus. God too gave us his 'one and only Son'. Clearly John was wanting his readers, who knew their Old Testament, to be thinking of the Abraham and Isaac story as they thought about what it cost God to give Jesus to them.

'Take your son, your only son, Isaac, whom you love . . .' (Genesis 22:1). God is well aware of the extraordinary costliness of the request. He emphasizes just how much Abraham loves his son, and hints at the journey he has already come through in order to have Isaac.

Abraham did of course have another son: Ishmael, through Hagar, but he was not the child of the promise. Ishmael was not the son from heaven whom Abraham and Sarah longed for, but barely believed possible. The name Isaac means 'laughter', reflecting the incredulous joy that overwhelmed Abraham and Sarah as they cradled their heaven-sent son in their arms.

The moral issue

There was also a huge moral issue hanging over God's extraordinary request. We know from other Old Testament passages how much God detested the child sacrifices that surrounding pagan nations made to their gods (see Leviticus 20:1–5 on the abominable child sacrifices made to Molech). Yet here was God asking Abraham to make the greatest sacrifice imaginable – a sacrifice that was abhorrent even to think about.

And surely, if we feel the abhorrence of Abraham in even contemplating sacrificing Isaac, how much more horrific must it have been for God to sacrifice his one and only Son, whom he loved? In one sense, giving up Christ to death on a cross was 'unthinkable' to God. That is how dramatic and emotive and costly our salvation really is. God did the unthinkable to rescue you from judgment and make you his child.

> I wish people who so demean the wrath of God would understand that they are simultaneously demeaning the love of God for his Son. It's precisely in the outpouring of his wrath upon his Son that the Father loves his Son in our flesh, because he's been willing to be obedient to death, even the death of the cross. [2] *Sinclair Ferguson*

A father's emotions

Abraham, no doubt with his head bowed and his heart heavy, trudges with his son towards Mount Moriah. And as the emotions of the story build, you are struck by the sheer innocence of Isaac, not knowing where on earth his dad is taking him.

> Abraham took the wood for the burnt offering and placed it on his son Isaac, and he himself carried the fire and the knife. As the two of them went on together, Isaac spoke up and said to his father, 'Father?'
>
> 'Yes, my Son?' Abraham replied.
>
> 'The fire and wood are here,' Isaac said, 'but where is the lamb for the burnt offering?'
>
> (Genesis 22:6–7)

Abraham takes the wood and places it on his son's back. Cast your mind forward two thousand years and picture God placing the cross-beam on Christ's back. The same pathos that hung over Abraham and Isaac's conversation, hangs around the cross as well. How did Abraham feel as he had this gentle conversation with his beloved son, knowing he was about to stick a knife in him? There is a real tenderness about the language. Notice how many times the word father (twice) and son (twice) are used in this brief exchange. A father talking tenderly to a son he is about to brutally sacrifice. The emotions are almost unbearable.

The son's innocence

And Isaac's innocence adds to the pathos: 'Father . . . where is the lamb for the burnt offering?' You almost wince at the question. But the innocence of Isaac is foreshadowing (or pointing towards) the innocence of Christ, the other beloved

Son, the other miracle child sent from heaven. Yet Christ was not innocent in the sense that he did not know what would happen to him; unlike Isaac, he knew exactly what would happen at the cross.

He was so powerfully aware that the cross was his destiny that he predicted it three times to his disciples (see Mark 8, 9, 10), and then cried out to his Father in the garden of Gethsemane to relieve him of the awful cup of suffering he would face. So Christ was not innocent in the sense of being naive about the cross.

But he was morally innocent. And that is what makes the cross such an extraordinary sacrifice. For a just and holy God who loves good and hates evil, who is thrilled in every way with the character of his Son, to be willing to allow his innocent Son to bear so brutal a punishment for sins he had not committed in order to save guilty, rebellious creatures like us – that is a deep mystery. But it helps us understand the power behind 'God so loved the world that he gave . . . '

That is where this story of Abraham and Isaac climbing Mount Moriah together takes us. Two thousand years later another Father and Son would climb Calvary hill 'together', with tortured emotions. In Isaac's case, of course, the father did not ultimately have to wield the knife on his son. A ram, caught in the thicket, would be a substitute.

But at Calvary there was no ram substitute. Instead the Son becomes the sinner's substitute, dying as the innocent 'lamb of God', for your sin and mine. This is the price that Father and Son were prepared to pay to demonstrate God's love for us. It had been decided in the courts of heaven that this was the only way salvation could be won for a lost human race, as Cecil Alexander's great hymn reminds us:

There was no other good enough
To pay the price of sin;
He only could unlock the gate
Of heaven, and let us in.[3]

We often concentrate on the pain Christ went through, as nails as thick as tent pegs were driven through his wrists and ankles. But how often do we think of the Father's pain? The Father was not an uninvolved bystander at the cross. Isaiah 53:10 reminds us that 'it was the LORD's will to crush him and cause him to suffer'. Paul tells us in 2 Corinthians 5:19 that 'God was reconciling the world to himself *in* Christ'.

> The Lord Jesus could die on the cross a thousand times, yet no salvation would be accomplished until God in heaven was satisfied with what the Son had done. If the work of Christ is to be finished, it is essential that it be finished in the estimate of God.[4] *Alec Motyer*

The Father's pain

The cross caused the Father untold pain in a completely different way from the Son. Father and Son were utterly united in their mission of love, and both sacrificed something profound to save us. I can almost picture Abraham on Mount Moriah, very gently tying his beloved son to the altar with a crude rope, making sure it wouldn't rub against his skin too much, yet knowing all the while he is about to sacrifice him.

And I can picture the Father in heaven wincing as he watches Roman soldiers hoisting, through a series of ropes, his beloved Son's cross, and feeling the cross thud into the earth. Was the Father not cut to the heart as every sinew and nerve ending in his Son's body jolted when the cross dug into the ground? God covered the sky with darkness so that no-one could see what he was about to do to his beloved Son, to deal with your sin and mine once and for all.

And what must have gone through the Father's heart when he heard the cry of dereliction from the Son who had lived in perfect communion at his side for all eternity: 'My God, my God why have you forsaken me?'

Jesus, who had referred to God as 'Father' in his sweat-filled, blood-saturated Gethsemane prayer, does not now call God his 'Father'. Jesus, the Son of God, becomes the sin bearer as he represents, for those sacred three hours of darkness, everything that is vile and sinful about humanity.

And God has to look away from his Son. He cannot come to the rescue of his gasping, broken Son, because his Son, for the first and only time in eternity, has taken on himself all that is hideous to God. He became 'sin for us' (2 Corinthians 5:21).

What happened at the cross?

When we ask the question, 'What happened at the cross?', surely it is here we must start. Not with depersonalized doctrinal statements and cold logic. Not with a 'doctor's pre-scription' kind of gospel. But with a Father and Son utterly giving themselves, totally poured out, to 'save a wretch like me', as John Newton so powerfully expressed it.

Gaze into the mystery. Remind yourself of the cost of your salvation. What the Father and Son went through 'together' to know you and be known by you. On the one hand, the cross is wonderfully reassuring. How much must we mean to the Trinity, the three persons of the Godhead, that the Father and Son would put themselves through the trauma of the cross to rescue us and to adopt us as sons and daughters of

God? 'How great is the love the Father has lavished upon us' (1 John 3:1).

Paul's prayer for the Ephesians is that they would have the power, simply to grasp (for it takes a lot of grasping) 'how wide and long and high and deep is the love of Christ, and to know this love that surpasses knowledge – that you may be filled to the measure of all the fullness of God' (Ephesians 3:18–19).

It is a wonderfully liberating experience to know, to really know, that God loves you, that he has 'lavished' his love on you like a waterfall. He did not demonstrate this love by sending a letter; he demonstrated it with nails and thorns.

The theologian Karl Barth, a man with a most brilliant mind, who helped to rewrite the script for twentieth-century theology, was once asked by a reporter, 'What is the greatest thought you have ever had?'

Barth paused for a moment, and then replied with disarming humility, 'Jesus loves me, this I know, for the Bible tells me so.' Barth had grasped something of the truth of Ephesians 3. Of all the profound themes to meditate on, you will find none greater or truer or more satisfying than this thought: 'Jesus loves me.'

> While the cross speaks of a love that does more than we believed possible, and provides a cleansing from sin which we could never do, it also stands as a challenge to service.[5]
> A. St John Thorpe

The challenge

But alongside the wonderful reassurance that God loves us, there is surely also a deep, life-consuming challenge. Paul said, 'Christ's love compels us' (2 Corinthians 5:14). If the Father and the Son have poured themselves out so radically at Calvary, then surely there is a moral compulsion that drives all our Christian living.

To reduce Christianity to a brief prayer of commitment at the moment of conversion, and to live a lacklustre, unchanged life from that point on, is an appalling, unworthy response to the God of the cross. It is a travesty when you consider the passion God has 'lavished' on us.

When Moses was challenging the people of Israel on Mount Sinai to obey God's law, Exodus 24:8 tells us that he sprinkled them with blood. The blood was a reminder of their solemn oath that they would obey the God who had rescued them from Egyptian slavery through the blood of a lamb.

But we, as believers in Jesus Christ today, are sprinkled in a much richer blood. Not the symbolic blood of a lamb or a goat, but with what Peter calls 'the precious blood of Christ' – imperishable blood of more worth than all the silver and gold put together.

This is what motivates us to live lives that are pleasing to the Father. Not because it is our duty. Duty can become a cold and passionless word. But because 'Christ's love compels us'.

The blood of Jesus is so rich to me, the love of God the Father has so captured my heart, the Holy Spirit has so stirred my conscience, that I want to live every day in a manner worthy of the cross. That was what Paul said from his prison cell to the Philippians, as he was pouring his own life out for Christ, 'Conduct yourselves in a manner *worthy* of the gospel of Christ' (1:27).

And it is the most splendid, agonizing, blood-soaked, passion-drenched gospel imaginable. A gospel centred on a cross where a Father gave his Son for the sins of the world.

So next Sunday, when you stand to worship, don't just mouth the words and go through the motions. Also enter in with emotion. Your relationship with God should involve fiery, soul-stirring passion. 'Love is as strong as death', as the Song of Songs tells us. Certainly God's love is. You are singing to the God who gave his darling Son to die for you. So let your heart burst into song.

Questions

1. What difference does it make in your life to know that God loves you?
2. In what way can the cross challenge us when our discipleship becomes lacklustre?

Passages for further study

John 1:1–18; John 3:16–19, 31–36; 2 Corinthians 5:14 – 6:2.

The perfect storm

Most Christians don't get very excited about creeds (concise statements of Christian belief). A creed can sound like some kind of dry formula, to be repeated without any feeling or real thought. But at the heart of the message of the cross there is a powerful creed that the Spirit of God wants to burn on your soul.

1 Corinthians 15:3 is the bull's-eye of Christianity. It is a specially-crafted, precise summation of the heartbeat of the Christian faith. In fact Paul introduces this creed with deliberately solemn words: 'For what I received I passed on to you as of first importance.'

In other words, Paul did not invent this creed himself. It had already been carefully constructed by the apostles of the risen Christ, the Twelve, who had been hand-picked by Jesus to be living witnesses to his resurrection. Paul was late in joining that select group of apostles, and this sacred creed was handed down to him.

And the creed begins, 'Christ died for our sins'. The phrase is deceptively simple, but alongside God giving us his Son, this phrase represents exactly what happened at the cross. Our whole salvation depends on the truth of these words. In fact Paul tells his readers that their eternal destiny is determined by their acceptance of this creed; 'By this gospel you are saved, if you hold firmly to the word I preached to you. Otherwise, you have believed in vain' (1 Corinthians 15:2).

The bull's-eye of the gospel

So the stakes are high as we try to understand what it means when we say 'Christ died for our sins'. Strangely, one of the most important words in this statement is the little word 'for' (*hyper* in the Greek).

Murray J. Harris, the renowned New Testament scholar, writes that the Greek word *hyper*, 'Seems to have arisen from the image of one person standing or bending over another in order to protect or shield him'.[1] In other words, what Jesus was doing as he hung naked on the cross, was actually shielding us, protecting us from something. From what? It may seem strange to suggest it, but he was protecting us from the wrath of God. God sent Jesus to die on a cross to protect us from God's own wrath against us.

But how does that work? You might say, 'I really don't care. Leave that for the scholars to fight over.' But actually, we do have to care. Every ordinary Bible-believing Christian has to care, because this little creedal phrase is the centre of the gospel. It is the difference between eternal life and eternal death, heaven and hell. So we really need to care.

The danger of God's holiness

To understand the concept of the wrath of God we must first understand his holiness. Many Christians today have a shallow, one-sided view of God. They think about him through the lens of what Don Carson has called 'one single, controlling attribute: love'.[2] Even though we rightly revel in the love that God has demonstrated at the cross, we cannot limit God to simply being love, even if it is our favourite attribute.

At the beginning of the Ten Commandments, God warns his people not to make an idol out of him. They were not to carve an eagle representing God's wisdom or a lion representing God's strength, because if they did, they would be limiting God. They would be reducing him to only one of his attributes, and would end up with a very skewed picture of deity.

God is not just love, he is beauty, grace, mercy, justice, wisdom, and especially holiness. And it is the extent of God's holiness, the awesome magnificence of his moral perfection, that we need to get to grips with. We cannot understand the cross until we do. A key passage of Scripture that helps us understand God's holiness is that awesome scene from Isaiah 6.

Holy, holy, holy

Isaiah was the godliest man of his generation. According to ancient tradition, he was sawn in two for his zealous commitment to bringing the uncomfortable oracles of God to his disobedient people. He was the kind of man who would leave my paltry commitment to God trailing in the dust. Isaiah represents the best of us.

But Isaiah received his call to be a prophet when he saw a captivating vision of God's holiness that left him distraught in his spirit. This temple experience made him realize what a corrupt man he was, because he caught a glimpse, just a glimpse, of the glory of God. And we all need to go through that kind of stripping bare process, seeing our sinfulness in the light of God's glory, if we are to understand the passion of the cross.

Isaiah was in the temple that day to mourn the passing of a great king, Uzziah, who had died prematurely of leprosy for flouting God's holy standards.

> If we cannot see how ugly, how death-dealing, how God-defying sin is, we shall not see how utterly satisfying the cross is, by which men and women alone are reconciled to God.[3] D. A. Carson

Degrees of holiness

But as Isaiah knelt to pray, probably for God's direction on the national life of Israel, he was caught in a trance and saw the true King of glory in all his heavenly splendour.

In the year that King Uzziah died, I saw the LORD seated on a throne, high and exalted, and the train of his robe filled the temple. Above him were seraphs, each with six wings: With two wings they covered their faces, with two they covered their feet, and with two they were flying. And they were calling to one another:

'Holy, holy, holy is the LORD Almighty;
   the whole earth is full of his glory.'
(Isaiah 6:1–3)

These seraphs (seraphim in older translations) in Isaiah's vision are the peak of the angelic host. Their name in Hebrew means 'burning ones' because they surround God's throne and are continually being burned up by God's 'glory', the outward manifestation of his inward perfection. God is so holy that he shines.

Clearly there are degrees of holiness. Even subordinate angels are called holy – morally pure. But these aren't subordinate angels, but burning seraphs, the highest angels in glory, the peak of creaturely perfection. Yet even they have to cover their faces and feet from the awesome glory of God.

When the normally understated Scriptures repeat a word three times to emphasize its intensity, you need to sit up and take notice. 'Holy, holy, holy is the LORD of hosts!' (verse 3, King James Version). God is not just good. He is not just very good. He is not merely holy, like the lower class of angels he created. Nor is he holy, holy, like burning seraphs.

God is holy, holy, holy. He is blazing in his glory, the sum of all perfections. And his holiness is dangerous – that's the point of Isaiah's vision. So dangerous in fact that the very pillars of the temple, and Solomon's temple had substantial pillars, began to shake at the presence of his majesty.

A ruined prophet

And Isaiah, the best man among us, the man who came to pray for his nation in the temple, feels the sheer radiance of God's glory like a scalpel cutting open his soul. He cannot take it. The full extent of his sinful heart is laid bare before the glory of God and he cries out, 'Woe to me! . . . I am ruined!' (verse 5).

If Isaiah felt 'ruined' by God's glory, then where does that leave you and me? We may not like to think of ourselves as 'ruined', but that is exactly where we stand before a God as intensely holy as Yahweh. And God's holiness makes every shade of sin that he sees in our hearts utterly heinous to him. That is the horrible truth we need to grasp.

Nobody wants to talk about it today, and fewer and fewer preachers want to preach about it, but our sins are horrendous to God. Every shadow of sin is unspeakably awful to him. That is why God appears so harsh in banishing Adam and Eve from his presence for a single misdemeanour – eating the forbidden fruit.

If I had been the judge in that scenario, I would have given Adam and Eve a slap on the wrist and told them to try better next time. But I am not three times holy. I do not shine with glory. Angels don't cover their faces in my presence. Sin in the Bible is not defined by what I find acceptable, but by what a white-hot-holy God finds acceptable. Sin is sin because God is God.

And God's holiness means he gets angry any time he sees a sinful act or a sinful thought, or hears a sinful word being spoken. If we are to understand the cross and what it took for *this* God to forgive sinners, we've got to get away from *our* view of sin and learn to appreciate God's view of sin.

The beginning of the gospel

God is angry at sin – every shade of sin. And when Paul begins to explain the gospel in the book of Romans, it is not the love of God he points to, but this difficult concept of the wrath of God: 'The wrath of God is being revealed from heaven against all the godlessness and wickedness of men' (Romans 1:18).

If there is one concept that we need to get into our heads before we can properly understand the cross, it is this notion, so foreign to our culture, so unpopular even in our churches, of the wrath of God. What happened at the cross of Christ is intricately tied up with God's wrath against our sin. We cannot understand the most basic confession of Christian belief, 'Christ died for our sins', until we get to grips with God's wrath.

Beautiful but dangerous

In 1997 Sebastian Junger wrote a book called *The Perfect Storm*, which was later turned into a Hollywood blockbuster movie. The book was based on real events that took place in October 1991, off the east coast of America. A storm front like few had ever witnessed hit the coast.

To be more accurate, an accumulation of three different, equally powerful storm fronts came together in an unprecedented way. The phrase the 'prefect storm' that inspired the title of the book was coined by the national weather service in America which had studied the storm.

From a meteorological perspective, the storm was a thing of great beauty. Weather round the east coast of America is particularly lively in the October/November season, as cold air coming down from Canada collides with the warmer air rolling in from the Atlantic. Hurricanes and cyclones are regularly created, but none as fearsome as the three storm fronts that came together on the fateful night of 28 October, 1991.

The perfect storm, beautiful though it was to meteorologists, was devastating to the boats that were caught in its deadly eye. Sebastian Junger's book follows the crew of a trawler, the *Andrea Gail*. This trawler was full of seasoned fishermen who had seen all kinds of difficult conditions at sea.

But nothing had prepared them for the perfect storm and its 100-foot-high waves. All six members of the crew, despite their maritime skill and experience, perished, missing presumed dead, and all that was found of the wreckage were a few fuel drums, a fuel tank and an empty life raft. The perfect storm was also the deadly storm.

And that is a picture for us of the wrath of God. God's holiness in itself is a thing of beauty – ravishing moral beauty that literally makes his being shine. But when that moral beauty collides with our sin, it creates the perfect storm: the wrath of God.

God does not get angry like we do. His wrath is not the irrational outburst of an unbalanced temper. Quite the opposite, God's wrath is the consistent response of his holy character to any and every shade of sin. As John Stott puts it in his Romans commentary, 'his wrath is his holy hostility to evil, his refusal to condone or come to terms with it, his just judgment upon it'.[4]

We should actually praise God for his wrath – his absolute antipathy to sin. It does not make life any easier for us, but the consistency of God's moral excellence is what makes God so beautiful, and therefore so angry when he sees sin.

God cannot and will not ever stop being absolutely morally perfect. And therefore he cannot and will not ever come to terms with our sin or lower his standards to let us into heaven by the back door. God is light, as 1 John 1:5 tells us, and 'in him there is no darkness *at all*'.

So let's go back to our creed and understand exactly what we need to be protected from. As it stands, we are sinners whose sin arouses God's wrath and makes us ripe for judgment. Hell is the place where God will pour out all his righteous wrath on sinners. Now I don't like that thought any more than you do. But the question is not, 'Do I like it?', but 'Is it true?' If we really understand God's holy character, it must be true. Hell is logically consistent with a holy, holy, holy God and his righteous hatred of sin.

But here is the glory of the cross. God, in his amazing grace, has dealt with his own holy hatred of sin in a way that rescues us from horrendous judgment. God chose to pour out his wrath on Jesus instead of us. And Christ was willing to pay that awful price.

All this amazing truth is hidden in the creedal phrase, 'Christ died *for* our sins'. Christ is the one 'bending over us' to shield us from the wrath of God. He is the shock absorber.

> In the cross God has satisfied his perfect and holy justice by executing the punishment our sins deserve. Without that, he would not be true to himself. And in the cross he pardons those who believe in Christ, even though they have sinned and deserve condemnation. Without this, we as sinful men and women would be excluded from his presence forever.[5] *Alistair Begg*

Propitiation

Graham Kendrick's song 'Come and see' talks about God's wrath and mercy meeting at the cross. At the cross God displayed his wrath against sin to its fullest extent. He gave us a picture of hell. But hanging there taking my hell, exposing his body and soul to the full force of God's anger against a whole history of human sin, was Jesus Christ, my sinless substitute.

God did not go easy on sin at the cross. How could a white-hot holy God ever go soft on sin? If he did, he would stop being God, the sum of all perfections. But somehow, at the cross, God's holiness collided with his love. God's wrath was met head on by his mercy, because he loves poor, guilty wretches like us. His love is as ferocious, as unbounded, as relentless as his holy hatred of sin.

So, as a demonstration of his relentless love, God made Christ a propitiation for our sin. If you don't know that word yet, learn it, and pray it back to God as an act of worship. Jesus is your propitiation, and propitiation means to appease someone's wrath. Jesus allowed the full, Niagara Falls force of God's anger against sin to fall on him during those three hours of Calvary darkness.

Wrath absorber

All the anger that was stored up in God's holy heart, against child molesters and rapists, against gossips and busybodies, against the odious proud and the corrupt hypocrite, God let it out all in a mighty torrent on the innocent flesh of his darling Son.

Here is how Charles Spurgeon described it in one of his sermons:

> The heart of Christ became like a reservoir in the midst of the mountains. All the tributary streams of iniquity, and every drop of the sins of his people, ran down and gathered into one vast lake, deep as hell and shoreless as eternity. All these met, as it were, in Christ's heart, and he endured them all.[6]

The Son felt the Father's rage. And if Jesus has taken God's wrath on my behalf, if he has stood in the gap as my divine substitute, then there is no wrath left for me: 'There is now no condemnation for those who are in Christ Jesus' (Romans 8:1).

What a beautiful, rugged redemption. God has not lowered his gloriously holy standards one iota. He is still the three times holy God of Isaiah's temple, who must punish sin in all its guises. He *must* be angry at my sin. But he has chosen to pour out that anger on his beloved Son.

And so, at one and the same time, God demonstrates his holiness and wrath: he pours out his anger at my sin. God demonstrates his justice: he has not left sin unpunished, because he has condemned Christ in my place. But God demonstrates his mercy by withholding from me the judgment I deserve, and his grace by pouring on me the blessings of forgiveness I do not deserve.

> There's not just one aspect to what Christ did on the cross. If I can put it in popular jargon, on the cross our Lord Jesus was 'multi tasking' and it's important for us to recognize that. So for example in Romans, Paul speaks about what happened on the cross as propitiation, expiation, redemption, reconciliation and so on. He understands there is something being effected in the death of Christ that is multi-levelled in its ability to deal with the multi-faceted consequences of Adam's fall and our sin.[7] *Sinclair Ferguson*

A robust cross

This is what saddens us about Christian teachers today who try to diminish all the implications of God's holiness, denying the difficult notion of the wrath of God, saying that the wrath of God is a pagan concept that we must reject. They end up with a flimsy cross that is a pale reflection of the real thing.

Some Christian writers and speakers have said that Christ's death is simply about his tremendous self-sacrifice. The cross is, of course, a wonderful act of self-sacrifice, but if you miss the wrath-absorbing power of Christ's death, you miss the very heartbeat of the gospel.

Richard Niebuhr famously summed up the skewed view that people end up with when they do not take the holiness of God seriously: 'A God without wrath brought men without sin into a world without judgment through the ministrations of a Christ without a cross.'[8]

If you are to gaze at the beauty of the cross, like an unfurled tapestry, you must hold on to this notion of propitiation. Hold on to Isaiah's vision of the blazing glory of God and the ruined prophet. Hold on to this idea that God is enraged by human sin because of his unsullied perfection.

And then fall down on your knees and marvel at the extent of God's love, that he would appease his own just, holy wrath through the sacrificial death of his Son. The cross is ghastly-yet-glorious. Its glory shines through its ghastliness.

Look at the broken, bloody, deformed, naked, ruined body of the spotless Son of God. That's how horrific your sin and mine is to a white-hot-holy God. That's how ferocious God's righteous anger really is, because that's how ravishing his white-hot holiness really is. Don't tone it down. Let the lion roar! Because love dwells here.

Real love

This is not the pale love of a valentine card or a wistful emotion, but the full blooded-love of a wrath-absorbing Saviour. The apostle John calls propitiation the very definition of love. 'In this is love, not that we have loved God but that he loved us and sent his Son to be the propitiation for our sins' (1 John 4:10, English Standard Version).

Revel in the peace that trickles from Christ's gaping wounds into your soul. God's righteous wrath against me has been appeased – propitiated. I am free to live as a blood-bought child of God. His holiness is no longer a threat to me. Unlike Adam, I don't need to hide behind the bushes when the Lord God walks in the garden in the cool of the day. Instead, I can come and meet my Saviour as a forgiven, accepted son or daughter. Hallelujah! 'Christ died for our sins.' Praise God for his wrath-absorbing sacrifice!

There is, dare we call it, a community plan on the part of the Father, the Son and the Holy Spirit. The Son is sent into the world to bear our humanity, to become the second Adam. What Jesus came to do was to undo what Adam did. The second man does what Adam failed to do: he lives a life of wholesome obedience to his Father. The second Adam bears the consequences of what the first Adam did and so he necessarily comes under the judgement and wrath of God.[9] *Sinclair Ferguson*

The call to holiness

But as we rightly revel in the price God was willing to pay to deal with his own holy anger at our sin, surely we must feel the urge to be holy in our hearts, by the Spirit's power. God has not removed his holiness to save us. He is as holy and as wrathful against human sin after the cross as he was before.

There is no contradiction between the God of the Old Testament, who leaves Isaiah trembling, and the God of the New Testament, who saves us in Christ. We have not been saved 'easily'. God's love for us is not a shallow thing where he simply decides to lower his glorious standards. Propitiation has shown us that there is no diminishing in God's white-hot glory.

So as Christians today, we should be constantly thankful for the wrath-absorbing love displayed at the cross, but also have a deep awareness that we are dealing with the same God who made Isaiah tremble.

This God has fiery eyes that stare through the curtains of our soul. Hebrews 12:29 reminds New Testament, cross-centred believers that 'our God is [still] a consuming fire'. He is still 'holy, holy, holy', and we should approach him each day with 'reverence and awe'. The fear of the Lord, as Proverbs puts it, is the beginning of wisdom.

The unsettling story of Ananias and Sapphira (Acts 5:1–10), carried out in body bags for secretly withholding money from the apostles, shows us a God who is still as holy and demanding as he ever was. Believers in Corinth 'falling asleep' (dying) because they disrespected the Lord's Supper (1 Corinthians 11:30) remind us that we cannot enter God's presence in a slapdash, casual manner, or feel that the cross means God has gone 'soft' on sin.

'Be holy to me, because I, the LORD your God, am holy' (Leviticus 20:26; 19:2) is as much a command for New Testament saints as for Old Testament Israelites. Look after your thought life in a polluted world filled with television and internet images programmed to leave your holiness in tatters. Feed your soul on good discipleship books, Christian biographies that show how the greats of the past (Jonathan Edwards, Amy Carmichael, Dietrich Bonhoeffer and Hudson Taylor) battled for holiness in a fallen world. And above all, read and meditate on the word of God, which washes you clean.

> Only when we truly realise the wonder of Christ will we truly hate sin, turn from that which is wrong and that which we know is wrecking us and our world.[10] *Chris Byworth*

The cleansing word

A father once told his son to collect water in a bucket from a local stream. But there were holes in the bucket. The boy went backwards and forwards several times to the stream, but by the time he got back to his father, the water had drained out.

The son protested, 'Dad, what's the point of getting water from the stream? Every time I come back, there's no water left in the bucket.' The father replied, 'Yes, but look how clean the bucket is!'

Every time I listen to a sermon or read the word of God, there is so little of it I remembers, so much that seeps out of the bucket of my mind.

But I know that every time I read or listen to the word of God, God cleans the bucket. I don't have to remember it all, or retain it all, to know that I have been washed. And the challenge is to keep going back to the pure water of God's word and allow our souls to be washed in it, so that we are clean vessels, ready to be used by our 'holy, holy, holy' Master.

Questions

1. Why is an awareness of God's holiness so crucial to our understanding of the cross?
2. What can you do in your life to remind yourself constantly of the holiness/wrath of God?

Passages for further study

Genesis 6:9 – 8:22; Isaiah 53; Romans 3:21–26.

3

The headless snake

As a kid, I loved Mission Sundays, when missionaries on furlough [home assignment] brought special reports in place of a sermon . . . There is one visit I've never forgotten. The missionaries were a married couple stationed in what appeared to be a particularly hot jungle. I'm sure they gave a full report on churches planted or commitments made or translations begun. I don't remember much of that. What has always stayed with me is the story they told about a snake.

One day, an enormous snake – much longer than a man – slithered its way right through their front door and into the kitchen of their simple home. Terrified, they ran outside and searched frantically for a local who might know what to do. A machete-wielding neighbour came to the rescue, calmly marching into their house and decapitating the snake with one clean chop.

The neighbour reemerged triumphant and assured the missionaries that the reptile had been defeated. But there was a catch, he warned: It was going to take a while for the snake to realize it was dead.

A snake's neurology and blood flow are such that it can take considerable time for it to stop moving even after decapitation. For the next several hours, the missionaries were forced to wait outside while the snake thrashed about, smashing furniture and flailing against walls and windows, wreaking havoc until its body finally understood that it no longer had a head.

Sweating in the heat, they had felt frustrated and a little sickened but also grateful that the snake's rampage wouldn't last forever. And at some point in their waiting, they told us, they had a mutual epiphany.

I leaned in with the rest of the congregation, queasy and fascinated. 'Do you see it?' asked the husband. 'Satan is a lot like that big old snake. He's already been defeated. He just doesn't know it yet. In the meantime, he's going to do some damage. But never forget that he's a goner.'[1]

On the cross Satan was decisively defeated. He just doesn't know it yet.

The reality of Satan

The evidence for the existence of Satan, that rebellious angel whom God threw out of heaven, is all around us. The Bible calls him 'the prince of this world' (John 12:31), and like the snake in the missionary's story, he is still thrashing around causing devastation.

Satan's defeat was predicted as early as Genesis 3:15 when God told the serpent in the Garden of Eden, 'I will put enmity between you and the woman, and between your offspring and hers; he will crush your head, and you will strike his heel.' Jesus would be the one who would crush Satan's head.

And right from the beginning of Jesus' ministry that was his purpose and goal; 'The reason the Son of God appeared was to destroy the devil's work' (1 John 3:8). Jesus exorcized demons, healed diseases, raised the dead, calmed storms and preached the good news of the gospel proclaiming freedom from sin. And with each display of his power, he was literally setting people free from Satan's grasp and extending God's kingdom into Satan's territory.

Satan's defeat at Calvary

> For ever, now, the Cross stands to us as the place of deliverance, the place where sin's power was broken.[2]
> G. B. Duncan

Jesus' mission to defeat Satan culminated in the cross. Calvary was an unlikely place for victory. As Jesus hung in naked agony on the cross, the nails impaling his body and the crown of thorns piercing his head, victory seemed very far away. But in the unseen world, where the real wars are won and lost, Jesus was achieving a cosmic victory over sin, death, Satan and his demons.

Colossians 2:13–15 explains what was really going on.

When you were dead in your sins and in the uncircumcision of your sinful nature, God made you alive with Christ. He forgave us all our sins, having cancelled the written code, with its regulations, that was against us and that stood opposed to us; he took it away, nailing it to the cross. And having disarmed the powers and authorities, he made a public spectacle of them, triumphing over them by the cross.

Jesus' death wasn't defeat, but victory! Jesus' death appeased God's wrath, cancelled the charges God had against us, so our sins could be forgiven. We are therefore no longer in Satan's grip – by dealing with sin Jesus disarmed Satan's power. And the image in Colossians is of the complete and decisive victory Jesus achieved. When heroes returned from battle they led the captives in a victory procession. And in Colossians, Paul describes Jesus leading Satan and his demons in a victory parade – stripped of their powers, led in shame, helpless and forced to submit to the victory of Christ.

Death defeated

As the writer to the Hebrews says, Jesus' death defeated Satan and also Satan's power over our death.

> Since the children have flesh and blood, he too shared in their humanity so that by his death he might destroy him who holds the power of death – that is, the devil – and free those who all their lives were held in slavery by their fear of death.
> (Hebrews 2:14–15)

Jesus' victory over Satan is seen most clearly in his resurrection. Jesus had defeated Satan's power over death, death could not hold him, and as a result it has no hold over us either. The moment we trust in Christ, our eternal life begins. As Jesus himself said, 'I am the resurrection and the life. He who believes in me will live, even though he dies; and whoever lives and believes in me will never die' (John 11:25–26). Though our bodies may perish, they will one day be raised, and we will live forever with Christ. The cross means we don't need to fear death or what will happen beyond the grave. As Paul triumphantly declared,

When the perishable has been clothed with the imperishable, and the mortal with immortality, then the saying that is written will come true: 'Death has been swallowed up in victory.'

> 'Where, O death, is your victory?
>   Where, O death, is your sting?'
> (1 Corinthians 15:54–55)

The German pastor and martyr Dietrich Bonhoeffer summed up the difference Christ's death has made to our dying.

Whether we are young or old makes no difference. What are twenty or thirty or fifty years in the sight of God? And which of us knows how near he or she may already be to the goal? That life only really begins when it ends here on earth, that all that is here is only the prologue before the curtain goes up – that is for young and old alike to think about. Why are we so afraid when we think about death? ... Death is only dreadful for those who live in dread and fear of it. Death is not wild and terrible, if only we can be still and hold fast to God's Word. Death is not bitter, if we have not become bitter ourselves. Death is grace, the greatest gift of grace that God gives to people who believe in him. Death is mild, death is sweet and gentle; it beckons to us with heavenly power, if only we realize that it is the gateway to our homeland, the tabernacle of joy, the everlasting kingdom of peace.

How do we know that dying is so dreadful? Who knows whether, in our human fear and anguish, we are only shivering and shuddering at the most glorious, heavenly, blessed event in the world?

Death is hell and night and cold, if it is not transformed by our faith. But that is just what is so marvellous, that we can transform death.[3]

> Tell me, with whom did the victory lie? Was it with Satan? Oh, that was a short-lived and illusory hope! The victory lay eternally with the Son of God, because the Almighty Father looked down from glory and listened to the cry of His Son and heard Him say 'It is finished!'. . . And on the third day, with the cry of 'It is finished' still ringing in His ears, the Father cried 'Amen, it is finished,' and raised His son from the dead, giving us the token and the truth that the victory lies with the Christ of Calvary.[4] *J. A. Motyer*

'Now' but 'not yet'

So what is happening now? If Jesus defeated Satan at the cross, why is the devil still active in our world and why is the spiritual war still raging? We don't fully know why, but the Bible gives us at least two reasons. God is waiting so that more people may have the opportunity to hear and accept the gospel and become Christians (2 Peter 3:9). And also God has allowed this time of evil to prevail in order to refine our faith (1 Peter 1:6–9).

So at the moment we face twin realities: we belong to Christ and Satan is defeated, but Satan has not yet conceded defeat and we still need to stand firm against him. Theologians call this tension the 'now but not yet'. And in the run-up to Christ's second coming, the Bible indicates that Satan will ramp up his attacks on believers (2 Thessalonians 2:1–12). This news isn't intended to unsettle or alarm us, but rather encourage us to stand firm in God's truth.

The writer to the Hebrews explains heaven's perspective on this 'now but not yet' time.

Day after day every priest stands and performs his religious duties; again and again he offers the same sacrifices, which can

never take away sins. But when this priest had offered for all time one sacrifice for sins, he sat down at the right hand of God. Since that time he waits for his enemies to be made his footstool, because by one sacrifice he has made perfect forever those who are being made holy.
(Hebrews 10:11–14)

Unlike the Old Testament priests whose job was never finished, Jesus has sat down. His job is finished: his sacrifice for sin was a once-and-for-all act. In his death, Jesus defeated Satan. Now he is waiting for Satan to submit to his authority – till his enemies become his footstool. Although we can see evil raging all around us, the battle has been won and we are waiting for the final victory to be acknowledged by all. We are waiting until 'at the name of Jesus every knee should bow, in heaven and on earth and under the earth, and every tongue confess that Jesus Christ is Lord, to the glory of God the Father' (Philippians 2:10–11).

Jesus' life and resurrection, but most particularly his death, defeated Satan and made his ultimate destruction certain. Jesus exorcized demons, calmed storms, rose from the dead – all guarantees, tasters, that the final victory over Satan is assured. Like that snake in the missionary story Satan has been defeated, but he is still thrashing around, still not conceding defeat. As we can see all around us, Satan continues to oppose God, God's people and God's work in the world.

> Waiting for submission. Tell me, who waits for submission? Only the One who has already achieved the victory. It is utter folly to wait for submission if the battle has not been fought and won. Jesus at the moment is not fighting; He has no more fighting to do. No, not to lift a finger to defeat

Satan. He has no more fighting; He is only waiting. He sits at perfect rest on the right hand of God. At perfect rest so far as Satan and all his power is past, and He simply waits for the submission of defeated foes.[5] *J. A. Motyer*

What is Satan doing now?

Jesus may have sat down, but Satan certainly hasn't! He's at war with us and we need to arm ourselves against him. As Ephesians 6:10–12 says,

Finally, be strong in the Lord and in his mighty power. Put on the full armour of God so that you can take your stand against the devil's schemes. For our struggle is not against flesh and blood, but against the rulers, against the authorities, against the powers of this dark world and against the spiritual forces of evil in the heavenly realms.

Satan has a full armoury of tactics. In some parts of the world he is behind the persecution of believers. In the West his ploys are generally more subtle. Satan deceives us with lies – lies about God's goodness towards us when we're going through difficult times, lies about the truth of God's word, lies about our eternal security (John 8:44). He stands as our accuser before God, dredging up past sins to make us feel guilty and powerless for service (Zechariah 3:1).

Satan looks for ways to corrupt us with the allure of money, power and physical comforts so that our hearts waver in devotion to God. He also tempts us into evil (1 Thessalonians 3:5). He even sends his followers to infiltrate our churches, masquerading as spiritual leaders (2 Corinthians 11:4, 13–15).

Although we are not always aware of his activity, the spiritual conflict is relentless. The 'prince of this world' is still thrashing about trying to destroy those who belong to Christ and blinding the eyes of unbelievers to the truth of the gospel (2 Corinthians 4:4).

Resisting Satan

So, what should our strategy be? How can we protect ourselves from the wiles of the evil one? Well, first we need to have a proper estimation of Satan's power over us. Remember, Satan has no claim on us. We are no longer slaves to sin, so we don't need to succumb to his schemes. Paul assures us that 'he [God] has rescued us from the dominion of darkness and brought us into the kingdom of the Son he loves' (Colossians 1:13).

> One sacrifice for sins forever; that is what Jesus has done. What a claim! That sin has finally and fully been dealt with. What a claim! And what a promise! That God, looking at us through the spectrum of Calvary; looking at us, His believing people, He holds out to us this promise and assurance, 'As far as I am concerned your sins are dealt with.' One sacrifice for sins, no matter how completely you discern yourself to be a sinner in need of forgiveness: one sacrifice for sins forever, so that to you, God Himself is offering an eternity on the basis of the finished work of Christ. What a claim, and what a promise![6] *J. A. Motyer*

We also need to remind ourselves that the devil's power is limited to what God permits. In the Old Testament, Satan challenged the motives for Job's righteousness and was allowed to test him – but only within the boundaries God set

(Job 1:12; 2:6). And the same is true for us. Satan cannot do anything to us without God's permission.

Sometimes God allows Satan to try us because he wants to prove our faith (1 Peter 1:6–7). Just think of Paul, who was given a 'thorn in [his] flesh, a messenger of Satan' to torment him. Perhaps this was some sort of physical infirmity. Whatever it was, he asked God to take it away, but God refused, reminding Paul, 'My grace is sufficient for you, for my power is made perfect in weakness' (2 Corinthians 12:7–9).

God also allowed Simon Peter's faith to be tested to prove it was genuine (Luke 22:31–32). Sometimes God allows Satan to afflict us in order to discipline us (Hebrews 12:4–11). But we need to remember that the devil will not have the final word. The devil cannot harm us in any ultimate sense since our lives are 'now hidden with Christ in God' (Colossians 3:3).

To counteract the devil's tactics we need to be active in resisting him, being fully aware of the particular temptations and weaknesses we are prone to and guarding ourselves against them. As J. C. Ryle comments,

> We are too apt to forget that temptation to sin will rarely present itself to us in its true colours, saying, 'I am your deadly enemy, and I want to ruin you forever in hell.' Oh no! Sin comes to us like Judas, with a kiss; like Joab, with outstretched hand and flattering words. The forbidden fruit seemed good and desirable to Eve; yet it cast her out of Eden. Walking idly on his palace roof seemed harmless enough to David; yet it ended in adultery and murder. Sin rarely seems [like] sin at first beginnings. Let us then watch and pray, lest we fall into temptation.[7]

Whenever we recognize sin in our lives we must be ruthless in dealing with it, nipping it in the bud. Ephesians 4:26–27 tells us not to allow anger to fester because that gives 'the devil a foothold' – it allows him into our lives to cause even greater sins and more hurt and harm. Instead of giving the devil a free entry pass into our lives by gossiping and slandering one another, we should occupy ourselves with God-honouring activities (1 Timothy 5:13–15), be disciplined in our devotion to God (1 Peter 5:8), read the Bible and meditate and pray through Scripture like Jesus did (Matthew 4:1–11), ask for God's help (Matthew 6:13), and hold on to God's promises (2 Peter 1:3–4).

We need to be vigilant, wake up to the cosmic conflict we are involved in and look out for the devil's advances. Where are your weak points, areas the devil habitually targets, and how can you strengthen them? Take action to stop believing the devil's lies: that you are excluded from Christian service because of a past sin, that God doesn't really love you, or that God owes you an easy ride because of all your service for him.

Ephesians 6:10–18 encourages us to put on the armour of God, daily clothing ourselves with God's protection, so that we can withstand the enemy's assault. That means each day being conscious of, and grounding ourselves in, God's truth and righteousness (verse 14). We should be ready to share the gospel, exercise God-given faith (verses 15–16), becoming sure of our salvation, knowledgeable and reliant on the Scriptures (verse 17) and prayerful (verse 18). If we do these things, we will have God's strength to resist the devil.

Satan's future

Although Satan is still thrashing about, wielding his powers, seeking to destroy us, his final destruction is certain. At the end of redemption history the devil and his angels will be thrown into a lake of fire (Revelation 20:10).

Until that day, God's kingdom is extended as we live faithfully for Christ. God's kingdom is built as people accept the good news of the gospel, as we comfort the broken-hearted, look after the poor and lonely and continue Jesus' mission on earth.

The refrain of Revelation 2 – 3 is 'to the one who is victorious', or, 'overcomes', and with God's help and strength we can be 'victorious'. Despite the vilest tactics of the devil, the cross means that the rallying cry of those first-century believers can be ours too. Through the blood of the lamb we shall overcome.

'So then, dear friends, since you are looking forward to this, make every effort to be found spotless, blameless and at peace with him' (2 Peter 3:14).

Questions

1. In what ways is the devil attacking you now? What lies is he telling you? In what ways is he tempting you? How can you resist him?
2. In what ways are you extending God's kingdom and taking territory off Satan?

Passages for further study

Matthew 4:1–11; James 4:1–10; Revelation 12:7–12.

Part two:
What difference does the
cross make to me?

4

Justification: A righteousness from God

Have you ever been struck by lightning? That was the frightening experience that drove a young German Catholic called Martin Luther towards life as a monk in a monastery. As legend would have it, the lightning did not actually strike his body, but hit the earth nearby, forcing him to the ground. He was terrified, and cried out a prayer to St Anne, promising to devote his life to God.

But his commitment to monastic life did nothing to quell his fear of God. It wasn't that he lacked the appropriate zeal – by his own admission, if anyone could have gained salvation through 'monkery', it was Luther. He was as disciplined and zealous a monk as could be found in medieval Europe.

But throughout all his disciplined spiritual exercises, Luther felt a deep unease in his spirit, for how could a sinful man ever stand before a righteous God? It seems strange in our twenty-first-century culture, where there is so little fear of God, to hear the thoughts of a man who was afraid of the righteous requirements of God.

But as Luther presided over the mass, filling his mind with thoughts of the glory of God and the unreachable heights of God's holiness, he would often tremble. How could his meagre spiritual disciplines catapult him to the heights of God's glory?

Luther's disquiet only intensified when he paid a visit to Rome itself, the Mecca of the Catholic Church. He had high hopes before his trip that the glory of the church in Rome, the eternal city, would inspire him and he would not feel so crushed about his own standing before God.

But when he saw the downright debauchery and seedy living of some of the bishops and even archbishops in Rome, he felt deeply troubled. He famously climbed Pilate's stairs, kissing every step as a matter of tradition, but pondering to himself where on earth he could find an answer to the dilemma raging in his soul.

Galatians and Romans

Luther's quest reached crisis point when his mentor back in Germany, a monk called Staupitz, asked him to teach a class on Galatians and Romans. And as Luther cracked open Romans 1, and began to study the text, the phrase 'the righteousness of God' seemed to scream at him.

The book of Romans was all about the righteousness of God. And this is the phrase that made his heart tremble: 'For in the gospel a righteousness from God is revealed' (Romans 1:17).

Wasn't this Luther's precise problem? If the gospel revealed God's righteousness, what hope did he or anyone else have? How can we ever attain to the righteousness of God? But as Luther read on, a spark was lit in his heart that would change the face of Europe, and eventually the world.

What we now call the Protestant Reformation was set in motion by Luther's careful study of Romans 1:17. As Luther read the whole verse, it became a balm to his soul: 'For in the gospel a righteousness from God is revealed – a righteousness that is by faith from first to last, just as it is written, "the righteous will live by faith".'

Here lay the answer to Luther's struggle. Yes, God was supremely righteous – it was right to fear him. It was right to ask the troubling question, 'How can sinful men and women reach the exacting standards of the righteousness of God?'

But there was a glorious answer. The gospel was all about a righteousness that God gives us as a free gift. It isn't something we can earn or a standard we have to reach. We don't have to shave our heads, commit ourselves to a monastery and focus on doing spiritual exercises. What a breakthrough that was! Luther's glass ceiling had been shattered.

Justification

So, God offered righteousness as a free gift. And this gift could not be obtained by filling our lives with enough good works to earn God's favour, for how would we ever know if we were good enough? It was obtained by faith alone, simply by believing in what God had done for us through the life, death and resurrection of Christ. How this doctrine works itself out is what we call 'justification by faith alone'.

The word 'justification', so central to Paul's argument in both Romans and Galatians, means 'to be declared righteous'. Paul is at pains in Romans 1 to 3 to describe how the whole world needs to be righteous to be acceptable to God. But none of us, not even one, can reach those standards.

Paul first runs his eye across the pagan world that has rejected God and descended into all kinds of immorality, envy, strife and jealousy (Romans 1:18–32). It has clearly fallen short of God's glory.

But that was not the shocking part of Paul's assault on the sinful human race. He claims that even outwardly moral people, people like the average good-living citizen, who might agree that complete pagans fall short of God's glory, are themselves no better (Romans 2:1–16). Even the best of us is still a sinner.

If we could attain righteousness by our own efforts, if we could reach a state of sinless perfection where everything we ever did, thought or said was pleasing to God, then God would commend us on judgment day. But even those people who strike us as moral, with wholesome family values, who put their loose change into the Salvation Army box – even they are lost in sin.

The sins that make us fall short of the glory of God are not simply the ones that send people to prison: murder, rape, stealing. The average 'good-living' person compares his or her life to the dregs of society and *feels* justified. But in actual fact, he or she is as much in need of God's righteousness as the drug addict shooting heroin on the street corner.

God despises pride, envy, jealousy, gossip, greed and lust – the socially acceptable sins that we do not call sin, but which are grievous in the sight of a holy, holy, holy God. In fact, he despises every act, even a seemingly good act, that does not have as its end goal the glory of God.

We were made for God's glory and we sin when we do not give God the glory he deserves as our supreme and righteous Creator. Remember Isaiah's vision? We don't compare ourselves to others. We compare ourselves to the God of burning holiness, before whom every shade of sin is heinous. The bar is outrageously high!

> When they executed a man in Edinburgh, they put up
> the notice 'so and so was justified at the Market Cross
> this morning at 8 o'clock' – 'justified' – paid the penalty,
> executed, slain for his sin . . . so the sinner who has died
> is regarded as having been justified. The account is settled,
> there is no charge against him, it has been paid and
> discharged; so when I see Christ dying for me, I know
> that my claim is settled, that I have died, and God
> justifies me gratuitously in the riches of his grace.[1]
> *George Goodman*

The religious

Paul then turns his attention beyond the pagan world and the outwardly moral world to the religious world, especially that of the Jew (Romans 2:17–29). Jews thought of themselves as the chosen ones, the world's teachers. After all, they had been given the law of God, the Ten Commandments, written on stone tablets by the very finger of God.

If anyone could declare himself righteous, surely it was the religious Jew with all his history, tradition and heritage! But Paul's damning indictment of the whole human race reaches its crescendo as he tells the Jews that they are perhaps most guilty of all. Ouch!

Yes, they have the Ten Commandments, but they do not obey them. Do those who claim to teach the world not teach themselves? The religious world with all its ritual, tradition and 'bells and smells', is no closer to God's righteous requirements than the average pagan.

And no religious ritual can wash away the deep stain of sin that dogs even the most zealous worshipper. Paul's conclusion is emphatic, 'Jews and Gentiles alike are all under sin . . . There is no one righteous, not even one' (Romans 3:9–10).

Every single member of the human race is on a level playing field before God. Whether we are a priest serving mass in a glorious cathedral, or a prostitute selling our body on a street corner, we all fall short of the glory of God. We all desperately need this gift called righteousness.

Jesus our righteousness

That's where Jesus comes in. For Jesus, as we know, has lived a perfect life of obedience. He is the only truly righteous human being who has ever lived: 'This is my beloved Son in whom I am well pleased.' Jesus' whole mission was to live the ideal human life, as a representative human being, so that his obedience to God, his record of perfect submission to God's will during the thirty-three years of his life, could be 'transferred' to us.

And so what Martin Luther called the 'great transaction' can take place through Christ's death on the cross. I am utterly helpless as things stand; I am depending on the righteousness of another.

And Romans is very clear: God offers me 'a righteousness that is by faith from first to last' (Romans 1:17). Wonder of wonders, I receive this gift simply through faith in what Christ has accomplished on the cross. The moment I believe that Christ died for my sin, the moment I ask for his forgiveness and invite him to be my Saviour, this great, invisible transfer takes place.

All my sin and shame, all the ways in which I fall short of the glory of God, all my record of pride and greed and lust and envy and gossip – my entire record of sinfulness – all is placed to Christ's account as my sin bearer. He is judged in my place at the cross.

In a sense, God has brought my day of judgment forward. He has already judged my sin by judging Christ, my divine substitute. And in exchange, God 'imputes' me with the righteousness of Christ. Christ's record of perfect submission to God's will, perfect obedience to God's law, is given freely.

I am clothed in the righteousness of Christ. So as God looks on my heart today, he no longer sees the sin that offends his holiness. If he did, I would have to be condemned. Instead, he sees Jesus. As another great hymn puts it,

> Because the sinless Saviour died,
> My sinful soul is counted free;
> For God the Just is satisfied
> To look on Him and pardon me.[2]

Every time I fail God, take a wrong turn, rouse his anger against my sin, God looks into my heart and sees the righteousness of Christ staring back at him. He looks at his perfect Son and freely and justly pardons me.

> Satan comes, in our imaginations, into the courtroom, and he says to the Father, 'Look at that sinner, how can you declare him justified?' 'Well, yes,' says the Father, 'they are a sinner. The charges that you bring are valid, but will you look at my Son's hands? And look at my Son's feet? And will you look at the wounds in my Son's side? Who are you to condemn? It is Christ who justifies.'[3] *Alistair Begg*

The wonder of justification

Justification does not mean that I am perfect in a practical sense. I am still in a sense as much a sinner the day after I am justified, as I was the day before. Justification is a legal transaction that has been made in heaven, whereby God considers me righteous 'in Christ'.

That is such an important phrase, repeated almost two hundred times in the New Testament. A Christian is 'in Christ', covered by the righteousness of Christ. The Reformers had a little phrase in Latin that sums up the position of the justified man or woman: *Simul justus et peccator* (at the same time righteous and a sinner). Isn't it thrilling? You begin to realize that the cross of Christ is all about God's grace towards us.

All human religion is ultimately built on the premise of adding up all our good works or performing the right religious rituals to earn our place in glory. The cross is the exact opposite. It is about God's grace achieving for me what I could never achieve under my own steam. As the preacher Vance Havner put it, 'Every religion says "do, do, do". The cross says "done"!'

I was very moved to read the conversion story of John Bunyan, the author of *The Pilgrim's Progress*. Bunyan had lived a retrograde life before committing himself to Christ, but his discovery of justification changed everything. This is how he described his conversion experience.

> But one day, as I was passing into the field . . . fearing lest yet all was not right, suddenly this sentence fell upon my soul, 'Thy righteousness is in heaven;'. . . I saw with the eyes of my soul, Jesus Christ, at God's right hand; there, I say, is my righteousness; so that wherever I was, or whatever I was doing, God could not say 'He wants my righteousness,' for that was just before him. I also saw that it was not my good frame of heart that made my righteousness better, or my bad frame of heart that made it worse; for my righteousness was Jesus Christ himself, 'the same yesterday, and today, and forever'.[4]

Not performance-based religion

Justification is a wonderfully freeing truth. Because this gift of righteousness is based on God's grace, not my merit, I do not need to worry about my own performance. We all have good days and bad days – days when our attitudes or actions make us hold our heads in our hands. But my justification never wavers depending on how much I have served God this week, or even how confident I feel about my own salvation.

I have counselled several people who have gone through bouts of real depression in their lives. Martyn Lloyd-Jones, one of the great justification preachers, wrote a book called *Spiritual Depression*, based in part on his own experiences. Many godly Christians go through psychological black holes, where either the chemistry of their bodies or Satan's personal attack makes them doubt their salvation. If our salvation depended on our roller-coaster emotions and whether we 'feel' saved or not at any given moment, we would surely be in a sorry state.

Thank God our justification is not based on our own emotions or performance, but on Christ's perfect performance. He is my righteousness and his righteousness is perfect, complete, fixed and eternal. Throughout the countless ages of eternity, Christ's perfect sacrifice will still be justifying me in God's presence.

So I don't need to worry about losing my salvation. I need have no fear that ongoing failure in my life places my salvation in jeopardy. It does not depend on *my* performance, but on *his*.

No guilt in life, no fear in death

My justification also releases me from the chains of a guilty past. How many, young Christians in particular, feel they cannot serve Christ with passion? They cannot put themselves forward in some kind of leadership capacity in a church because of some past sin – problems with pornography, perhaps sleeping with a girlfriend or boyfriend. They feel in their hearts that they have crossed a line that means they can never be worthy, frontline servants of Christ in the future, so it is better just to keep their heads down. If you find yourself in that situation, remember your justification.

John Piper talks about Satan winning two victories: the victory that made you fall to that past sin and the victory that makes you feel your past failure disqualifies you from any meaningful future service. But take a good look at the kind of people who were considered heroes of faith in Scripture, God's front-line lieutenants.

Think of Moses the murderer, David the adulterer, Abraham the wife swapper, Peter the denier, Thomas the doubter, and perhaps especially, the man whom God called to preach this gospel of grace around the world, Paul the terrorist. That religious bigot, who killed Christians for a living, is the man whom God called to reach the Gentiles for Christ, to preach the message of justification to the world. Here was a man whose sins were so grievous that the first Christians were terrified of him when news reached their ears he had been converted.

> Here are the major fruits of our justification – peace with God (which we have), grace (in which we stand), and glory (for which we hope).[5] *John Stott*

It is noteworthy that in all of Paul's writings, he hardly ever harks back to the days of his anti-Christian terrorist activities. He never wakes up in the middle of the night with sweaty palms wondering if his assenting to the martyrdom of Stephen (Acts 8:1) barred him from the gates of heaven.

Okay, he knew he was 'the worst' of sinners (1 Timothy 1:15), but he boasted in the grace of God expressed in his justification, and frequently laid out his apostolic credentials to churches who doubted them. Lesson: don't let guilt from past sins blunt your willingness to serve God today in frontline Christian ministry.

As Jesus pointed out to Simon the Pharisee, it is those who know they have been forgiven much who love much (see Luke 7:36–50) and become the most effective Christian leaders – trophies of God's grace. That is the freedom that justification brings.

Christ centred-gospel

So don't beat yourself up about past sin. Don't keep dredging up what God has already cast into the deepest sea. Just rejoice in Jesus your justification. Robert Murray MacCheyne, the great Scottish pastor, said, 'For every one look at yourself, take ten looks at Christ.'

That is Christian living in a nutshell. The gospel is so Christ-centred. He is its architect, its procurer and its goal. Paul sums it up, 'Christ Jesus has become for us wisdom from God – that is, our righteousness, holiness and redemption' (1 Corinthians 1:30).

Don't get down about your performance. Rather, let the frustration of your fallen heart lead you to worship Jesus all the more. God looks at him and pardons you. It does not honour Christ for you to be weighed down about past sins he has already dealt with. Instead, it is far better to look to the sky and see your righteousness standing at God's right hand:

My sin – O the bliss of this glorious thought! –
  My sin, not in part, but the whole,
Is nailed to His cross, and I bear it no more:
  Praise the Lord, praise the Lord, O my soul![6]

Questions

1. How would you answer someone who said 'God is unjust to forgive sinners'?
2. In what way does the doctrine of justification contradict 'performance-based religion'?

Passages for further study

Romans 1:16–17; 4:1 – 5:21; Galatians 3:6–14.

5

Redemption: Set free to become what we are

In the 1970s Bob Dylan wrote a song called 'You gotta serve somebody'. It's not often that we get our theology from pop lyrics, but Dylan summed up the state of humanity well. He said that it didn't matter if we were an ambassador, the heavyweight champion of the world, a socialite, a preacher, a barber or somebody's mistress – whatever our social status or accomplishments, we all have to serve somebody.

We may assert our independence, fight to defend our rights and get our own way, but Dylan inadvertently points to a key biblical truth. We are all dependent creatures; we're all 'gonna have to serve somebody', and the only choice is who. The Bible says we are either serving God or Satan; we are either slaves of Christ or slaves to sin (Romans 6:16). And that transition, that change of master from Satan to Christ, is only possible because of the cross. Our escape from sin's grasp and our freedom to serve God could only be achieved through Jesus' death. The Bible calls this transaction 'redemption'.

Nowadays redemption is a word we generally hear only in church, but for the early Christians it was quite common.

In ancient times, economic circumstances such as a bad business deal or the death of a breadwinner often forced people to put themselves into slavery. This was a desperate measure. The only hope a slave had of being released was if a friend or relative paid the ransom price to their master. Once the ransom price was paid, the slave was set free. They were taken out of the marketplace, no longer viewed as a commodity and treated once again with dignity.

Slaves to sin

We've already seen that, like the first-century slave, we are in a hopeless state. We don't like to admit it, but from the moment we are born Satan has mastery over us and we are slaves to sin. As Charles Wesley's famous hymn 'And can it be' puts it: 'long my imprisoned spirit lay, fast bound in sin and nature's night'. Sin was part of my nature, my DNA, and I couldn't do anything to release myself from its grip.

Our two older boys are big fans of the Star Wars movies. And in Star Wars there is a huge space station called the Death Star which has a tractor beam that drags in enemy ships. Any smaller ship that gets too close to the Death Star gets caught up in the tractor beam. No matter what the ship does, there is no chance of escape; the ship cannot do anything but be pulled into the space station. That is the kind of power sin had over me before I believed in Jesus. Sin had me in its tractor beam. I couldn't help sinning. I was programmed for selfishness and had little clue how to obey God.

Before we became Christians we were all in that hopeless state. There was nothing we could do to restore our relationship with God. We needed a rescuer, a redeemer – someone to pay the ransom price to set us free.

From his earliest days Jesus was described as our Redeemer. Simeon and Anna in the temple recognized that he was the one who would bring redemption to Israel (Luke 2:30–32, 38). And Jesus himself recognized that our redemption was his mission in life. He said, 'The Son of Man did not come to be served, but to serve, and to give his life as a ransom for many' (Mark 10:45). Paul explains that 'Christ redeemed us from the curse of the law by becoming a curse for us, for it is written: "Cursed is everyone who is hung on a pole"' (Galatians 3:13). The law said we were law breakers because of our sin and attitude towards God, and the penalty for that was death. By taking our place on the cross, Jesus paid the ransom, released us from the penalty of the law and declared us right before God.

We cannot push the ransom analogy too far and ask to whom the redemption price is paid – the Bible never addresses this issue. All we need to know is that the ransom paid was priceless:

> For you know that it was not with perishable things such as silver and gold that you were redeemed from the empty way of life handed down to you from your ancestors, but with the precious blood of Christ, a lamb without blemish or defect.
> (1 Peter 1:18–19)

A new master

Our costly redemption means that we have a new master; we have been transferred from the kingdom of darkness to the kingdom of light (Colossians 1:13–14). This doesn't mean that sin no longer affects us. Martyn Lloyd-Jones famously used an illustration of two fields to describe our relationship to sin. I used to live in the field where Satan and sin controlled my life. But now I have been lifted out of that field and placed in a field where Christ and righteousness control my life. I can still hear Satan's seductive voice over the wall, but my goal now is to move further and further away from the wall where I can hear him.

Romans 6 outlines this reality. As Paul explains, on the one hand God has accomplished a decisive break with sin on our behalf: 'You have been set free from sin and have become slaves to righteousness . . . You have been set free from sin and have become slaves of God (Romans 6:18, 22). But on the other hand, we need to continue to fight the war against sin and keep ourselves from being affected by it.

> In the same way, count yourselves dead to sin but alive to God in Christ Jesus. Therefore do not let sin reign in your mortal body so that you obey its evil desires. Do not offer any part of yourself to sin as an instrument of wickedness, but rather offer yourselves to God as those who have been brought from death to life; and offer every part of yourself to him as an instrument of righteousness.
> (Romans 6:11–13)

Jesus' death on the cross has set us free from the penalty of sin and made us 'slaves of God', but each day we still need to resist the power of sin and the desire to serve our former master.

The great enemy of the Gospel puts the question to us every day, 'Shall we continue to sin?' How do you answer the devil? I hope you begin with an outraged negative: 'God forbid!' But I hope you go further than that, and that you confirm your negative with a reason. Because there is a reason, a solid, logical, irrefutable reason why the subtle insinuations of the devil must be repudiated. The reason is based on what we are. We are one with Christ (Romans 6:1-14), and we are slaves of God (Romans 6:15-23). Our Christian conversion has had this result: it has united us to Christ, it has enslaved us to God.

Now, what we are has these inescapable implications. If we are one with Christ – and we are – then with Christ we died to sin, and we live to God. If we are enslaved to God – which we are – then *ipso facto* we are committed to obedience. It is inconceivable that we should wilfully persist in sin, presuming on the grace of God. The very thought is intolerable.

You and I need to be talking to ourselves, and saying, 'But don't you know that you are one with Christ; that you have died to sin, and risen to God? Don't you know that you are a slave to God, and committed therefore to obedience? Don't you know these things?' And go on asking yourself that question until you reply to yourself, 'Yes I do know. And by the grace of God I shall live accordingly.'[1] *John Stott*

Counting ourselves dead to sin

Like newly-freed slaves in the first century, we take a while to get used to our new status and behave like slaves of Christ rather than slaves to sin. Theologians call this process 'becoming what we are', and it starts with counting ourselves dead to sin. This does not mean pretending that sin does not exist or that we are perfect, but acknowledging that through Jesus' death on the cross our debt to sin has been paid, the law has been satisfied, Satan's claim on us is over, the bonds of sin have been broken, we have a new master and are free to live a new life in Christ.

At its most basic level, 'counting ourselves dead to sin' means trusting that Jesus' death on the cross was sufficient to forgive our sins. This is the essence of redemption, the forgive-ness of our sins (Ephesians 1:7; Colossians 1:14). It is one thing to say that our sins are forgiven, but quite another to live out the reality of forgiveness. Sometimes we feel powerless to change sinful habits, locked in as we are to self-destructive patterns which we hide from others. We tolerate our sin, enjoy it at times, even though we know it saps our strength for ministry and makes us feel empty. Jesus declared, 'It is finished', but we don't know what freedom in Christ really means; we feel bound by sin and guilt.

It may not seem a nice comparison, but we're a bit like circus elephants! When they are young they are trained by being attached by heavy chains to large stakes driven deep into the ground. They strain and struggle, but the chain is too strong, the stake too rooted. One day they give up, having learned that they cannot pull free, and from then on they can easily be 'chained' with a slender rope. When this enormous animal feels any resistance, though it has the strength to pull the whole circus tent over, it stops trying, still believing it is bound by the heavy chains. We need to stop acting as if we are bound by the chains of sin, because the reality is that Christ's death broke those chains. Sin is still in our world, but through the Holy Spirit's power we can overcome it; we can pull free.

Becoming what we are

Living out our new freedom as slaves of Christ should be obvious to others as our priorities, values and attitudes shift to become those of Christ's. As Romans 6 explains, we need to have a two-pronged attack to tackle sin and 'become what we are'. One element is actively rooting out sin in our lives, not giving it oxygen to live and grow. We need to be intentional about protecting our thought-life and what we allow our mind to dwell on, as well as being wise about where we go and the activities we get involved in.

Spiritual maturity will not happen simply by avoiding sin, so we also need to be positively pursuing holiness: 'offer every part of yourself to him [God] as an instrument of righteousness' (Romans 6:13). This starts by spending time with God daily in the Scriptures, in prayer, asking for the Holy Spirit's help to behave like God's children.

When my brother, sister and I (Elizabeth) were young, my father would always encourage us to behave well in public by saying to us, 'Now remember who you are and who you belong to.' And essentially that is what we have to do as believers. Daily we need to spend time with God, remembering we belong to him and what it cost to redeem us. We need to let these realities motivate us to live up to our status as children of God. We will not behave like the redeemed without trying. Conquering sin is a daily struggle, a battle of the will. As Don Carson explains, 'People do not drift towards holiness. Apart from grace-driven effort, people do not gravitate towards godliness, prayer, obedience to Scripture, faith and delight in the Lord.'[2]

'Yield your members as instruments' – your bodies, your bodily members, your mental faculties. God needs your eyes, through which to look out with compassion upon the world; with a compassion that will care enough, it may be, to go, to speak, or to pray. God needs your feet, to carry the message of His concern and the message of His grace. God needs your hands, to toil, and by their touch reveal His love. God needs your lips, to speak for righteousness and truth. God needs your mind, to conceive ways by which the needs of the world might be met. God needs your heart, to throb with concern and compassion. God needs you.[3] *George B. Duncan*

Pursuing holiness

We need to be pursing holiness by having a daily 'quiet time' when we read our Bible and pray, by reading good discipleship books rather than watching mindless TV, by listening to sermons and worship music, by meeting up with other Christians to pray. As Paul said, 'Whatever is true, whatever is noble, whatever is right, whatever is pure, whatever is lovely, whatever is admirable – if anything is excellent or praise-worthy – think about such things' (Philippians 4:8). And as we pursue holiness, the Holy Spirit, whose power raised Jesus from the dead, promises to work in us to transform us and make us more like Christ (Ephesians 1:17–20). The question we need to ask ourselves is: do we love Jesus enough, are we passionate enough about his glory to fight against sin and pursue holiness?

Becoming a Christian and being redeemed mean bringing every area of our lives into conformity to Christ and his commands. There is no halfway house and nothing is off limits. We are slaves of Christ 24/7, and he has purchaser's rights. Our devotion isn't Sundays only with five weeks annual leave. As slaves of Christ we are chained to him and to his commands: to love our neighbour, to be devoted to our marriage partner, to meditate on God's word, to tell others about Jesus, to be pure in our thought-life, to surrender our money and possessions to God. Being redeemed means we allow Christ mastery over every area of our lives. As Paul said, 'You are not your own; you were bought at a price. Therefore honour God with your bodies' (1 Corinthians 6:19b–20).

In Old Testament times, every seven years Hebrew slaves were set free from their masters. But just occasionally there was a slave who loved his master so much that he chose to commit himself to that master for life. The slave would go through a special ceremony to mark this commitment when his ear would be pierced with an awl (Exodus 21:2–6). In the same way we are slaves of Christ and God invites us to dedicate ourselves to serve our heavenly master for life.

Will you make or renew that commitment today? Are you willing to say 'Pierce my ear, Lord. I want to be exclusively devoted to your service for the rest of my days'?

The bigger picture

Our redemption, however, has a wider focus and a greater impact. 'Christ loved the church and gave himself up for her to make her holy . . . to present her to himself as a radiant church, without stain or wrinkle or any other blemish, but holy and blameless' (Ephesians 5:25–27). Christ has redeemed not just individuals, but the church. What does that mean for us? Well, we need to treat one another as 'blood-bought' brothers and sisters. If Jesus loved the folk in your church enough to die for them, then you need to view them as precious. We need to get rid of back-biting, gossip and character assassinations over coffee. We need to build one another up with our words and actions, carry one another's burdens and seek one another's good (Ephesians 4:29; Galatians 6:2). We need to devote ourselves to the church – the people and its work – because Christ gave himself up for her.

Taking the long view

'Becoming what we are' is not an immediate transformation. The discipleship journey lasts a whole lifetime. And despite our best efforts, the trajectory to godliness is not usually a steep curve. More often than not, our spiritual lives, though generally making progress, are full of peaks and troughs. We will not always behave like the redeemed – there will be times when we walk too close to the fence, to use Martyn Lloyd-Jones' analogy. It is then that we must come back to the cross for strength and forgiveness.

But as we strive to 'become what we are' and live as slaves of Christ, we can look forward to the day when our redemption will be complete. The Bible talks of a future day of redemption (Ephesians 4:30) when our Redeemer will return to the earth (Job 19:25; 1 Thessalonians 4:16) – a day when we will be free from the presence of sin, our bodies healed of sickness and disease, and there will be no more temptation, pain or tears. We will be made perfect (Romans 8:23). Until that day we must keep coming back to the cross: the pivotal moment in redemption history, a guarantee both of what God has done and what he will do. The cross points back to what Jesus' blood has accomplished – our debt of sin cancelled, our forgiveness complete and our new status as slaves of Christ achieved. The cross also points forward to the culmination of God's redemption plan when world history will be wrapped up, Satan's rule will end and Christ will reign forever.

> And so when I say to you, 'yield yourselves unto God, as those that are alive from the dead, and your members as instruments of righteousness unto God,' I am asking you to do the most wonderful, the most glorious thing you could ever do. And also the most urgent thing that the church of Jesus Christ and the Head of the church needs today. This is precisely where the church has failed. We are not yielded to God.[4] *George B. Duncan*

Questions

1. How would you explain the concept of redemption to a non-Christian?
2. Do a spiritual inventory. Over the past month how effective have you been at tackling sin in your life? What measures have you taken to pursue holiness? Are you nearer this month to 'becoming what you are'? What further action do you need to take?

Passages for further study

Psalm 130; Hebrews 9:11–15; 1 Peter 1:17 – 2:3.

6

Reconciliation: Bridging the great divide

'Here's the gospel: you're more sinful than you ever dared believe; you're more loved than you ever dared hope.'[1] These twin themes of our sinfulness and God's love are the heartbeat of the cross. The Bible says we were 'God's enemies', 'alienated from God' (Romans 5:10; Colossians 1:21). God's burning holiness meant he could not look on our sin, and we could not stop sinning, so our relationship with him was irretrievably broken. That's why we need Calvary.

Restored to God now

We don't have to wait until heaven to enjoy a restored relationship with our heavenly Father. The moment we trust in Christ, we have peace with God (Romans 5:1) and full and free access to him through prayer. We can approach God without any fear of recrimination or guilt; as Paul says, 'he has reconciled you by Christ's physical body through death to present you holy in his sight, without blemish and free from accusation' (Colossians 1:22).

> On the cross as Jesus cries out from that agony of desolation, 'My God, my God, why hast Thou forsaken me?' He is cut off from God – by our sin. That, says Paul, is where the reconciliation has been accomplished. That is where he has found the love of Christ, and it set his heart on fire, beloved. He entered into all that it meant to be isolated from God, even for these moments which were an eternity, in order that we might know what it was to be brought nigh, and brought back, and know that fellowship with the Father for which we were born. That is the work of Christ for us.[3] *Eric Alexander*

The splitting of the temple curtain from top to bottom was a tremendous visual portrayal of the access to God we now have (Matthew 27:51). The cross means that God's presence is no longer reserved for priests only, but open to all who believe in him. Charles Wesley's hymn sums it up well:

No condemnation now I dread;
Jesus, and all in Him, is mine;
Alive in Him, my living Head,
And clothed in righteousness divine,
Bold I approach the eternal throne,
And claim the crown, through Christ my own.[4]

> You have been delivered out from the curse, the wrath and the condemnation, into the grace of access to God. You are justified from all things, and now a new life of access to God is open to you. The king has pardoned you and released you from prison, and now he invites you into the palace. You have been delivered out from condemnation, and you have been delivered into fellowship with God.[5] *Theo. M. Bamber*

Hope for the future

And the benefits of reconciliation don't stop there. With reconciliation also come a God-based confidence and hope for the future. Romans 5:10 explains 'For if, while we were God's enemies, we were reconciled to him through the death of his Son, how much more, having been reconciled, shall we be saved through his life!' We can have great confidence that our salvation is secure. If the death of Christ reconciled us to God, then surely the living Christ will keep us reconciled. And if God reconciled us to himself while we were his enemies, how much more will he do for us now we're friends?

Pastor John Piper explained it this way to the children in his congregation,

> Children, imagine you move with your parents into a new neighborhood. And during the first night a fire breaks out in your house. Your neighbor – let's call him Mr. Peterson – sees the smoke, calls the fire department, breaks a window, wakes everybody up, crawls inside, gets your mom and dad to safety, but they have passed out. He hears you calling from an upstairs bedroom before the fire fighters arrive. He dashes up the stairs, wets a blanket in the bathtub, plunges through flames in the hall, wraps you in the blanket and brings you safely outside with terrible burns on his arms and face. Over the next months you become very close friends with your Mr. Peterson and visit him in the hospital.
>
> One morning after he gets home, you ask him, 'Mr. Peterson, will you come over this afternoon and show me a new trick with my yo-yo?' Mr. Peterson says, 'Sure, I'd love to.' But during the day you start to wonder if he will really come. And you say to your father, 'I'm not sure Mr. Peterson will come this afternoon. He might forget, or maybe he really

doesn't care about a little kid like me.' And then your father says, 'You know what? If Mr. Peterson was willing to run through fire to save you at the risk of his own life and getting terrible burns, then how much more will he be willing to come over and show you a new yo-yo trick this afternoon! If he did the hard thing for you, then all the more surely, he will do the easy thing.'[6]

We can have confidence our salvation is secure. And because of that, no matter what suffering or sadness we endure in this life we can rejoice in God 'through whom we have now received reconciliation' (Romans 5:11). We can also rejoice now, whatever our current circumstances, because our God is completely trustworthy and our home in heaven is waiting for us. Look to the cross and find there an unshakeable confidence in God and a source of eternal joy which will undergird your life and keep your eyes on what really matters.

Maintaining the peace

But like any reconciled relationship, we will need to work hard to maintain the peace. It is not that we can break the bonds of reconciliation through our sinning, but we can certainly test them. In this respect, our relationship with God is like the relationship we have with our own children. No matter how naughty they are, our children will always be ours and we will love them, but bad behaviour certainly does strain the relationship! And the same is true of our relationship with God.

Our sinning will never break the 'salvation peace' we have with God, but we still need to make every effort to 'live at peace with him'. As Peter urged his readers as they thought about the return of Christ, 'since you are looking forward to this, make every effort to be found spotless, blameless and *at peace* with him' (2 Peter 3:14). If we deliberately keep on sinning and make no effort to address sinful habits and patterns of behaviour, then we make a mockery of Christ's death and show how little we think of his sacrifice. We will hurt him all over again. Instead, knowing how much our reconciliation cost and how much we have been saved from, we should strive to live 'at peace with God', reading his word, obeying his commands, fighting temptation, fleeing sin, listening to the Holy Spirit's promptings, frequently asking for forgiveness and seeking to please him and live out his values. Living a reconciled life is what it means to be a disciple, a follower of Christ.

Reconciled to one another

Being reconciled to God also changes our relationship with others. The film *Invictus* tells how Nelson Mandela, in his first term as President of South Africa, enthusiastically supported the nation's mostly white rugby team in an effort to bring about racial reconciliation in the country. But Mandela's efforts to eradicate apartheid did not stop with the rugby team. He sought every opportunity for reconciliation – even in the way he put together his security team. His black body-guards objected when Mandela sent white reinforcements to join their ranks – men who could well have been involved in the torture and death of their family and friends. Mandela stood his ground and replied, 'The rainbow nation starts here. Reconciliation starts here.'

And God says the same to us today: 'The rainbow nation starts here. Reconciliation starts here.' The book of Revelation looks forward to the day when heaven will be filled with people 'from every tribe and language and people and nation' (Revelation 5:9). There will be a rainbow nation in heaven because God accepts people of every colour and background. Reconciliation with him is not dependent on colour, gender, background or education. The only criteria with God are repentance and faith in Christ's work on the cross. And that means there should be no disunity, no hostility between different groups of people in our churches, because we have all been reconciled to God. The unity that will be evident in heaven needs to be worked out now.

Our reconciliation with others is the evidence that God has reconciled us to himself, the gospel is true and the Holy Spirit is at work in our lives. As Vinay Samuel, the Indian Christian leader and author, says,

> One sign and wonder, biblically speaking, that alone can prove the power of the gospel is that of reconciliation. . . . Hindus can produce as many miracles as any Christian miracle worker. Islamic saints in India can produce and duplicate every miracle that has been produced by Christians. But they cannot duplicate the miracle of black and white together, of racial injustice being swept away by the power of the gospel.[7]

Unity in practice

In the first century, reconciliation was most keenly seen in the unity between Jews and Gentiles. '[Jesus'] purpose was to create in himself one new humanity out of the two, thus making peace, and in one body to reconcile both of them to God through the cross, by which he put to death their hostility' (Ephesians 2:15–16). Paul goes on to say, 'Through him we both have access to the Father by one Spirit. Consequently, you are no longer foreigners and strangers, but fellow citizens with God's people and also members of his household' (verses 19–20).

The cross means that all believers are members of God's family, and it has achieved a unity which we must work out in practice. And this message resounds throughout Scripture:

> Here there is no Gentile or Jew, circumcised or uncircumcised, barbarian, Scythian, slave or free, but Christ is all, and is in all. (Colossians 3:11)

> So in Christ Jesus you are all children of God through faith, for all of you who were baptized into Christ have clothed yourselves with Christ. There is neither Jew nor Gentile, neither slave nor free, nor is there male and female, for you are all one in Christ Jesus. (Galatians 3:26–28)

It is obviously not the case that there are no actual differences between male and female, Jew and Gentile, but that those differences should not create division in the church. Hence the Keswick motto, 'All one in Christ Jesus'.

The cross of Christ destroys the dividing wall of hostility that alienates one person from another. God intended the church to be this new humanity, displaying his wisdom to the rulers and authorities in the heavenly realms (Ephesians 3:10). The church was God's best idea, his hope for the nations. Jesus didn't die so we could form a committee; he died to create a community – a community built on love, forgiveness, openness and self-sacrifice. His vision was for a community sharing each other's lives, not dominated by gossip but grace, a community demonstrating God's love to the world.

God's vision
So how does your church measure up to God's vision? We need to look at our churches – is there a sense of unity

between male and female, young and old, those of different backgrounds and education? Or do our personal desires for different worship styles, expectations about dress codes or assumptions about others drive a wedge between us? Do we reflect the diversity of our neighbourhood? Do we embrace other cultures and classes, or is it made painfully obvious to any newcomer that only like-minded people are accepted? To what extent is your church reflecting the reconciliation Christ won on the cross? Are we displaying God's desire for a unified church of devoted followers?

> In Ephesians 2, Paul points out that at the cross not only are we reconciled to God, but at the cross we are reconciled to one another; and that there He has made us one in the blood of the cross. All the divisions of mankind are done away with; and when this tent, with its title 'All One in Christ Jesus' becomes a real demonstration, and is poured out into the world, I believe Keswick will help the world to know today, as it has never known before, that here is a oneness in the family of God, which is one of the great messages of the cross.[8] *Philip Hacking*

It's personal

But reconciliation is not just the business of the church in general; it is personal. In the Sermon on the Mount, Jesus said,

Therefore, if you are offering your gift at the altar and there remember that your brother or sister has something against you, leave your gift there in front of the altar. First go and be reconciled to them; then come and offer your gift.
(Matthew 5:23–24)

Notice we are urged to take the initiative to reconcile, even if it is the other person who is holding the grudge against us. The Bible is saying that it is fruitless to worship God when we know about a broken relationship – being reconciled to God is meaningless if it doesn't affect our relationships with others.

We are not to let bitterness fester, but instead pursue peace at every turn. We are to make every effort to forgive, and ask for forgiveness, so that we can be reconciled with those whom Christ loves. This is hard work; it is painful, and involves us making the first move, but it is the hallmark of a disciple (John 13:35). Sadly, our testimony suffers when the world witnesses fighting and division within the church. And the church suffers too when believers deeply wound one another.

Of course there will be times when a person refuses to be reconciled with us, times when an agreement cannot be reached. Think of Paul and Barnabas, two godly men who could no longer work together in a joint missionary effort because they could not agree about John Mark accompanying them (Acts 15:36–41). Let's pray that our churches will be preserved from divisions like that. Let's be doing all we can to be reconciled with our brothers and sisters, as Paul exhorts us, 'If it is possible, as far as it depends on you, live at peace with everyone' (Romans 12:18).

Our ministry of reconciliation

Christ's work of reconciling us to God is finished. But while we can't add to what Christ has done, there is a sense in which the reconciliation process is ongoing. God has made us his ambassadors and given us the responsibility of sharing the gospel, because if the gospel is not preached, if the good news is not shared, if people don't repent, then they cannot experience reconciliation with God.

In his second letter to Corinth, Paul sets out these twin realities of Christ's finished work on the cross and our ongoing ministry of reconciliation:

> God . . . reconciled us to himself through Christ and gave us the ministry of reconciliation: that God was reconciling the world to himself in Christ, not counting people's sins against them. And he has committed to us the message of reconciliation. We are therefore Christ's ambassadors, as though God were making his appeal through us. We implore you on Christ's behalf: Be reconciled to God.
> (2 Corinthians 5:18–21)

God's ambassadors

We are all God's ambassadors, but being a foreign ambassador here on earth is a privilege only a few experience. When he was the Secretary of State during the Reagan administration, George Shultz kept a large globe in his office. When newly-appointed ambassadors had their first interview with him, Shultz would test them. He would say, 'You have to go over to the globe and prove to me that you can identify your country.' They would go over, spin the globe and put their finger on the country to which they were being sent.

When Shultz's old friend and former Senate majority leader Mike Mansfield was appointed ambassador to Japan, even he was put to the test. This time, however, Ambassador Mansfield spun the globe and put his hand on the United States. He said, 'That's my country.'

Shultz said, 'I've told that story, subsequently, to all the ambassadors going out. "Never forget you're over there in that country, but your country is the United States. You're there to represent us. Take care of our interests and never forget it, and you're representing the best country in the world."'[9]

Wherever we go in the world, wherever we serve, our role is to represent God and to take care of his interests. We have an amazing privilege because we are not merely representing the best country in the world (whichever that might be!), we are representing the King of heaven. For foreign ambassadors there is no down time, no moment when they stop being an ambassador, even when the gates of the embassy are shut. Likewise, we never stop being God's ambassadors.

Whatever we are doing, whether we are driving our children to school, leading a Bible study, or working in an office, we are God's ambassadors. We represent him, we show others what he is like, and we are to take care of his interests. To be good ambassadors we need to know God and to be growing in our relationship with him. We need to be Psalm 1 Christians, with our roots established in God and his word, or as Jesus describes it in John 15, we need to be connected to the vine. When that happens, through the Holy Spirit's power, we can live by God's values, promote his priorities and serve his agenda in every circumstance.

Speaking for him

But as the passage in 2 Corinthians 5 explains, representing God means we must also speak about him. We must be looking for opportunities to share the gospel with others (Colossians 4:5). Because if we don't, they will never know about what God has done for them. My father-in-law carries around small Christian booklets to give to people. He'll put one in the envelope when he's posting a bill; he'll give one to the checkout assistant at the supermarket. He is always looking for opportunities to speak about Jesus, to start a conversation. We are not all good with cold contacts, but if we are praying for God to use us, he will give us opportunities. For many of us heavily involved in church life, friendships with non-Christians may be quite limited, but we each have a sphere of influence – people we rub shoulders with every day, people we can invest in, build a relationship and share the gospel.

On one occasion, Billy Graham had just sat down after issuing a gospel invitation at one of his crusades. In that sacred moment of silence as individuals flocked to the front of the auditorium to respond to the invitation to become Christians, Billy Graham told the dignitary sitting next to him, 'I went to the hairdresser's today'. At first the man just ignored him, shocked that Billy Graham would be talking about such trivia at this holy time. But he said it again, 'You know, I went to the hairdresser's today'.

The man was about to ask him to be quiet when Graham added, 'and that lady coming to the front over there, she cut my hair'. Even when he wasn't on duty preaching, Billy Graham had a passion for the gospel, a desire to share the message of the cross, and this even extended to his hairdresser. We all have contacts like that: parents at the school gate, colleagues in the office, people in the gym. Pray that God would give us opportunities to speak to these people about the message of reconciliation.

> That is what your life is for; that God may make His appeal through you to the world.[10] *Eric Alexander*

The message of the cross

The cross is a profound symbol of reconciliation. It speaks of our reconciliation with God, won for us on the cross. The mission of Christ, completed at Calvary, means that reconciliation is ours to enjoy now – we have peace with God, our salvation is secure and we don't have to fear the final judgment. And the cross speaks not only of Christ's mission but our mission. Each one of us who has been reconciled with God is now his ambassador. There are no exemption clauses. We are to pursue reconciliation with other believers and represent God to the world, bringing his hope and truth to the nations. To whom are you holding out this precious word of life?

Questions

1. Think about your sphere of influence. Are there five unbelievers you know who you can pray for daily to become Christians? Pray for opportunities to share your faith with them.
2. What are you doing in church to promote unity? What relationships are you building with folk of a different age, different background, different Christian experience? How could you cross the barriers in your church and encourage true community?

Passages for further study

Colossians 1:15–23; Philippians 2:1–11.

Part three:
How can I live a cross-shaped life?

7

The crossed-out 'I'

Dr Helen Roseveare, a medical missionary in the Democratic Republic of the Congo, explains how she learnt about the cross-shaped life.

I was desperately overworked. I was the only doctor for half a million patients. There was no colleague to turn to, and all the responsibility fell on my shoulders. I had become quick-tempered and impatient with my colleagues – Africans and missionaries alike.

Fortunately for me my African pastor was watching me and saw my spiritual need. One Friday he came to my village and told me to pack my bags; I was going to spend some time in his village. I packed my rucksack, got my bicycle and cycled out behind him to his village. He had told his wife I was coming, and she had a room ready for me. Firmly, but courteously he said, 'Just get yourself in there and get yourself straight with God.'

Friday night, all day Saturday, Saturday night, all day Sunday, I spent before God. And I got nowhere. The heavens were like brass, the Bible was dead, I couldn't get through to him. By Sunday night I was depressed and discouraged, I had such a sense of failure; everything was so hopeless. I went to the door of the house and out in the courtyard, by the embers of the fire, sat my pastor and his wife. I went out and sat beside them. After a long, painful silence, I said, 'Please, help me.' My pastor leaned towards me and spoke patiently, 'Helen, do you know what's wrong with you? We can see so much Helen that we cannot see Jesus.'

He was silent for a while. And then, with his heel he drew a large capital 'I' in the dirt. Then quietly and deliberately he said to me, 'I think you know that person, don't you? "I" dominates your life. Me, my, mine; self – everything revolves around you – your program, your vision, what you want to do. Even when you hear on the news that some new law has been passed, the first thing you ask is, How will that disrupt my program? "I" is in the middle of everything.'

He said some other things that were very painful for me to take. I knew they were true, but I didn't realize he did. And then he seemed to change the conversation. He said, 'I notice that you drink a lot of coffee, and every time they bring you a cup of coffee you stand with it in your hand waiting for it to cool. May I suggest to you that every time you stand waiting for your cup of coffee to cool you just pray a short prayer. And as he said the words of the prayer, he drew another line in dirt across the first one. 'May I suggest that you pray, "Please God, cross out the I and make me more like you"'.[1]

In the dust of the African ground, Helen Roseveare learned the theology of the cross-shaped life. She called it 'The crossed-out-I life'. And that prayer 'Please God, cross out the I and make me more like you' is not just a prayer for missionaries or pastors, but for every disciple.

Take up your cross

Jesus said, 'Whoever wants to be my disciple must deny them-selves and take up their cross and follow me' (Mark 8:34). Today we often speak flippantly about 'having our cross to bear'. But when the Bible talks about carrying a cross it's not referring to a minor health struggle or difficult relatives. When a person carried a cross beam through the streets in the first century it meant only one thing – they were condemned to die and were on the way to their execution. When Jesus calls us to 'take up [our] cross', he is calling us to cross out the 'I', to put to death our own agenda and programmes, our sinful desires and our old self. As Paul said, 'those who belong to Christ Jesus have nailed the passions and desires of their sinful nature to his cross and crucified them there' (Galatians 5:24, New Living Translation). Imagine nailing your sin to the cross: your pride, your deceit, your lustful thoughts, your desire to be recognized. . . Imagining the horror of that crucifixion scene, all the pain and agony, helps us to begin to see just how much God hates sin, and how decisively and ruthlessly he demands that we deal with it.

Our 'cross-carrying' journey starts when we become Christians. When we first repented and asked God to be the Lord of our lives, we nailed our sinful nature to Christ's cross. However, 'carrying our cross' is not a once-in-a-lifetime event, but a daily non-negotiable for followers of Christ (Luke 9:23). As Paul explains, we have taken off our 'old self' but we have still got to put to death old habits:

> Put to death, therefore, whatever belongs to your earthly nature: sexual immorality, impurity, lust, evil desires and greed, which is idolatry. . . . You used to walk in these ways, in the life you once lived. But now you must also rid yourselves of all such things as

these: anger, rage, malice, slander, and filthy language from your lips. Do not lie to each other, since you have taken off your old self with its practices and have put on the new self, which is being renewed in knowledge in the image of its Creator. (Colossians 3:5, 7–10)

Saying 'yes' to Christ

At conversion we nailed our sinful nature to the cross and now we must continue being ruthless with sin. Every day we are confronted with a myriad of choices where we have the opportunity to say 'no' to self, my desires, my ambitions and selfishness, and 'yes' to Christ. It is much easier to live for yourself, to enjoy and indulge in selfish desires. But Paul urges us to 'train [ourselves] to be godly' (1 Timothy 4:7). He's asking us to discipline ourselves, to put in the effort, to renounce sin. And it's hard! It's painful to acknowledge and root out sin in our lives, to cross out the 'I'. Cross-carrying is costly – it not only involves self-denial but real suffering. This 'suffering' will look different to each one of us – isolation in our workplace, being misunderstood when we don't exert our 'rights', denying ourselves legitimate pleasures to serve God wholeheartedly, estrangement from family and friends, or in some countries, being persecuted by the government.

But we don't suffer alone; we don't strive to please God alone. Paul reminds us that we'll know 'participation in [Christ's] sufferings' (Philippians 3:10). We will know a greater intimacy, a richer fellowship with Christ when we suffer for his sake. Also, the Holy Spirit strengthens us as we carry our cross. He helps us say 'yes' to Christ and 'no' to self. As Romans 8:13 explains, it is only with the Holy Spirit's power we *can* live a crucified life: 'For if you live according to the flesh, you will die; but if by the Spirit you put to death the misdeeds of the body, you will live.' The Holy-Spirit power which raised Jesus from the dead is the same power at work in us every day, helping us to deny self and obey God (Ephesians 1:19–20).

Give me all

> Christ says, 'Give me all. I don't want so much of your time and so much of your money and so much of your work: I want you. I have not come to torment your natural self, but to kill it. No half-measures are any good. I don't want to cut off a branch here and a branch there. I want to have the whole tree down. I don't want to drill the tooth, or crown it, or stop it, but to have it out. Hand over the whole natural self, all the desires which you think are innocent as well as the ones you think are wicked – the whole outfit. I will give you a new self instead. In fact, I will give you myself: my own will shall become yours.'[2]

Carrying our cross means surrendering all that we are and have. This is the essence of Romans 12:1: 'Therefore, I urge you, brothers and sisters, in view of God's mercy, to offer your bodies as a living sacrifice, holy and pleasing to God – this is your true and proper worship.' Carrying our cross means we are that living sacrifice – our whole self devoted to God, living for his glory and bringing him pleasure.

> The great business of the Christian is not living but dying; not how to live a victorious Christian life, but how to negotiate a humiliating death . . . not a matter of deepening the spiritual life, but a matter of burial and death. At the risk of being misunderstood, may I suggest that you dismiss all your worries about not experiencing the victorious life: make it your concern to die. Your business, my business, is not

life, it is death. If I may say so reverently, our Lord's business is not life, it is death. God's business was resurrection. You may have come to Keswick seeking for life. Give it up! Occupy your mind with the question of how you shall die, and leave to God the business of how you shall be raised from the dead. If our Lord had said to the Father, 'What I am troubled about is how I shall be raised from the dead; how shall those strong Roman soldiers around the grave be dealt with?' the Father would have said: 'Leave that to Me; make it your business to drink the cup, to go to the Cross; Mine is the great task of resurrection.' And any Christian may be so obsessed, even to the point of mental, nervous and spiritual confusion, with the question of life without ever entering into the real question of death.[3] *Theo. M. Bamber*

Living the cross-shaped life

What does it mean for me?

What does the cross-shaped life look like in practice? What does it mean for me? It means that we model ourselves on Christ. His submission to God, humility and obedience were all-consuming, determining every thought and action. Paul tells us to

> have the same mindset as Christ Jesus:
>
> > Who, being in very nature God,
> > > did not consider equality with God something
> > > > to be used to his own advantage,
> > > rather, he made himself nothing
> > > > by taking the very nature of a servant,
> > > > being made in human likeness.

And being found in appearance as a man,
> he humbled himself
> by becoming obedient to death –
>> even death on a cross!
(Philippians 2:5–8)

When Jesus came to earth, he didn't push his own agenda, but delighted in pursuing God's agenda even when it cost him his life. And if the cross is to shape us, then it must shape our wills and bring them into line with God's. As we know, to know God's will we must spend time daily with him in his word, and then submit to its truth, obeying the commands of God, delighting in his promises, living by his priorities, promoting his values.

Money matters

This will have very practical consequences. Carrying our cross has implications for our finances, for example. Are we giving sacrificially to God? Is our lifestyle substantially different from our peers because we are investing heavily in kingdom ministry? In his article 'A Lot of Lattés', Ron Sider reviews the book *Passing the Plate: Why American Christians Don't Give Away More Money* and concludes,

> If just the 'committed Christians' (defined as those who attend church at least a few times a month or profess to be 'strong' or 'very strong' Christians) would tithe, there would be an extra 46 billion dollars a year available for kingdom work . . . $46 billion would fund each year 150,000 new indigenous missionaries; 50,000 additional theological students in the developing world; 5 million more micro loans to poor entrepreneurs; the food, clothing and shelter for all 6,500,000 current refugees in Africa, Asia, and the Middle East; all the money for a global campaign

to prevent and treat malaria; resources to sponsor 20 million needy children worldwide. Reasonably generous financial giving of ordinary American Christians would generate staggering amounts of money that could literally change the world.[4]

And the same must be said for the UK. If we are truly carrying our cross, it will have serious implications for our wallets and our bank balances.

Time and talents

The cross must also affect how we think about our time and talents. If all we are and have comes from God, if we are to be living sacrifices, then we need to see to it that our time and talents are completely devoted to his service. As we do our work and raise our children, are we doing it in God's strength and for his glory? In the daily routines of life we are called to live the life of Christ, not fritter away our time on worthless things, but be actively thinking how we can use our gifts and time to further God's agenda: what young people could I mentor in the faith, what older person could I show care to, what Bible study group should I attend, who could I pray for, what discipleship book should I read, what Bible verses should I memorize? A 'crossed-out-I life' means thinking how best we can put God first in the daily grind of life, but also asking the bigger questions: how am I investing in God's kingdom and what sacrifices am I making to further God's agenda here on earth?

One of my friends has a child in nursery. The teachers sent a letter home inviting any parent with a special talent to come in to speak to the children. Firemen, doctors, parents who had been to exotic countries, all shared their experiences with the class. My friend at first dismissed the letter, thinking she had nothing to contribute. But then she realized that this opportunity was an answer to her prayers. She'd been praying about how she could make a difference for God in the school community. So she offered to tell the Easter story, do crafts with the children and then give each one a book about the Easter story. For each one of us, life presents similar opportunities: occasions where we can use our time for God, serving his purposes rather than our own.

What does it mean for my family?

Home is where people see us raw. The mask comes off, and in our moments of relaxation and tiredness our family sees us as we really are. They bear the brunt of our bad habits and mood swings. But by the same token, our family should be the first to see the difference that carrying a cross makes. Living a cross-shaped life will revolutionize our marriages as we seek to love each other with Christ's love – a love which puts the other first, seeks the other's good, is quick to forgive and urges us towards godliness (Ephesians 5:21–33). What a testament at the end of your marriage to hear your spouse say, 'My husband/wife made me a better person and encouraged me to be a more devoted follower of Christ.'

A cross-shaped life also affects how we bring up our families: our goals for our children, the activities we support them in, the values we promote. It's right for us to be concerned about our children's health, their happiness, their education, but are we as concerned about their spiritual well-being? God has charged us as parents to invest in the spiritual lives of our children. We are to tell them about him, pray for them, be examples to them, help them make godly choices and cultivate their fledgling faith.

Because our children are masters of procrastination, spiritual conversations usually come at bedtime! At the end of a hectic day sometimes it's a struggle to summon up the energy and enthusiasm to spend time reading the Bible, praying with them and answering their elaborate questions. It takes self-denial on our part when we'd rather be downstairs with a mug of coffee! But there is no point in praying for my children's spiritual life if I am not doing anything about it. It's that daily, incremental spiritual investment into their lives that makes all the difference.

But our children need more than just to hear about the Christian faith – they need to see it lived out. They will be watching our lives closely – more closely than we think! – observing how we respond to God in the good and bad times. They are first-hand witnesses of our love for God, our trust in him and our obedience to his word. They will be the keenest assessors of whether our walk matches our talk. And if we want our children to one day carry their crosses, they must see us carrying ours. One of the things this means is that they grow up seeing me serving God in the church and kingdom ministry. Yes we want to spend time with our children, to bring them up well in God's sight. But that must not preclude our devoted service in the church. Our children must see us serving God in sacrificial ways, for how else will they know that God is worth everything?

> The real reason for trivial, superficial Christian living in ourselves and others is almost always a trivial, superficial view of the sin-bearing death of Jesus.[5] *Eric Alexander*

What does it mean for my church?
The Christian community is a melting pot of men and women from a variety of backgrounds, classes, races and cultures, all worshipping together. And as such, it provides many

opportunities for us to deny our own desires and rights in order to prioritize those of others. The Bible is full of verses about how we are to treat 'one another', such as, 'Be kind and compassionate to one another, forgiving each other, just as in Christ God forgave you' (Ephesians 4:32). And collectively, we submit our agenda to God's. As Colossians 1:18 states, Christ 'is the head of the body, the church'. In church we must set aside our own right to be heard and our desire to be recognized, in order that God's purposes may be served – the gospel preached, men, women and children saved, and us acting as salt and light as we serve our communities and show them what he is like.

In our churches, God's agenda must be most clearly seen in our preaching. Living a cross-shaped life means that the preacher is not at liberty to preach simply what he wants or what listeners will enjoy hearing. The preacher is constrained to preach the Bible, expounding its truths clearly. Paul explained that the gospel is our core message (1 Corinthians 15:1–11) and he outlined the centrality of the cross in his own life and ministry: 'For I resolved to know nothing while I was with you except Jesus Christ and him crucified' (1 Corinthians 2:2). As a congregation, we also have responsibilities. Carrying our cross means coming to church every Sunday, asking God to speak to us and being resolved to obey his word. Our weekly church attendance is not the end of our devotion, but rather an oasis from where we go out into the world encouraged, motivated and inspired once again to live the cross-shaped life.

Crossed-out-I life

A cross-shaped life is well described by Helen Roseveare's phrase 'the crossed-out-I life', because that is what it is.

Carrying our cross means submitting to God in everything and nailing our own desires to his cross. This is a daily challenge which requires perseverance and the Holy Spirit's power. Cross-carriers do not take holidays – wherever we are, whatever we are doing, each day we are to 'take up our cross' and follow Christ. It is the pursuit and purpose of our whole lives –what we were made for. And as we take up our cross we must make sure we are doing it for Christ's sake. We can't be involved in ministry or sustain self-denial if we are doing it simply to please others, to get noticed or maintain friendships, because ultimately we will be hurt and disappointed. The lynchpin of our crossed-out-I life is that we are doing it for Christ. And if we are doing it for him, then no sacrifice he asks us to make will ever be too big. As C. T. Studd said, 'If Jesus Christ be God and died for me, then no sacrifice can be too great for me to make for him.' Live the cross-shaped life and join the ranks of cross-carrying believers down the generations.

Do you see what this means – all these pioneers who blazed the way, all these veterans cheering us on? It means we'd better get on with it. Strip down, start running – and never quit! No extra spiritual fat, no parasitic sins. Keep your eyes on Jesus, who both began and finished this race we're in. Study how he did it. Because he never lost sight of where he was headed – that exhilarating finish in and with God – he could put up with anything along the way: Cross, shame, whatever. And now he's there, in the place of honour, right alongside God. When you find yourselves flagging in your faith, go over that story again, item by item, that long litany of hostility he ploughed through. That will shoot adrenaline into your souls!

(Hebrews 12:1–3, *The Message*)

No, there is no once-and-for-all blessing that relieves us from the need for daily trust and daily obedience and daily vigilance. But I do know this, that when I do rely on Christ crucified, not only for forgiveness but for strength, I am never let down. When I take my stand upon the burnt ground of the cross and resurrection, I am not defeated. When I rely on myself, I am. Christ crucified: I crucified. Therein lies the whole of the Christian life. Jesus crucified for me: that guarantees my pardon. I crucified with Christ: that is the pathway to power. Christ crucified for me: there I see God's total claim on my life, my self, my everything. I crucified with Christ: why, that is the only fitting response that a poor sinner can make to his crucified Lord.[6] *E. M. B. Green*

Questions

1. Are there any particular selfish desires, attitudes or habits that you know you need to nail to the cross? Spend time in prayer and repentance, asking the Holy Spirit to help you renounce these sins.

2. What practical steps could you take each day to remind yourself to live the crossed-out-I life? Some of the following may be useful: practicing moments of solitude, reciting a prayer, meditating on a particular Bible verse, including frequent times of confession to God.

Passages for further study

Matthew 6:19–24; Galatians 5:16–26; Philippians 3:7–14.

8

The fellowship of his sufferings

Many men owe the grandeur of their lives to their tremendous difficulties.

(C. H. Spurgeon)

One of the stand-out characters of my (Jeremy's) child-hood back in Northern Ireland, was a lady called Isa. She went to our little Gospel Hall in Larne. And I remember her so vividly because she was the first person I ever saw in a wheelchair.

Our communion service used to start at 11:30 on a Sunday morning, and with about five minutes to go, exactly the same ritual took place every week. Isa's sister would wheel her to about half-way up the sanctuary, and place her wheelchair at the end of the pew. Then she would open Isa's handbag, pull out Isa's little black Bible, because Isa was not able to do that herself, and place the Bible into the palms of Isa's frail hands. Isa had multiple sclerosis.

Today Isa is in glory, awaiting the new body she will be given on the Last Day. But during the fifteen years I lived in

Larne, I remember Isa being wheeled up to that same spot in church. I never knew her outside a wheelchair.

The other stand-out quality about Isa was her stunning smile. As I think of her today, I cannot picture her without her smile. A smile was permanently and radiantly stretched across her face. And every time I am thinking of groaning about some petty little inconvenience in my life, the vision of a beaming Isa in her wheelchair stops me short.

The problem of suffering

I have no category in my mind for people like Isa – one of the loveliest ladies you could ever hope to meet, a lady of powerful intellect, who was one of the best conversationalists I have known. What was God thinking when he wrote the script for Isa's life? When he put, in the early chapters of her life story, the title, wheelchair, the life sentence called multiple sclerosis? David teaches us that 'all the days ordained for me were written in your book before one of them came to be' (Psalm 139:16).

We cannot run away from the unsettling truth that for some of the wonderful Christians we know, God has written some of the most horrendous scripts. Perhaps yours is one of them. Why does God write some of the worst scripts for some of his best people?

No easy answers

As I write this chapter, I am very wary of giving you a 'neat-package' solution to this question of suffering that has troubled far greater minds than mine for centuries. Every Christian needs a category in their minds labelled 'mystery'.

The very character of God demands that label. God is limitless and undefinable. He says so himself. When he revealed his name to Moses, he called himself 'Yahweh', a name that is hard to grab hold of, almost impossible to define. 'I am who I am', or 'I will be who I will be'. The Hebrew can be translated either way.

The name is deliberately vast and unsearchable. And exactly how this timeless God sovereignly rules over all the puzzles and tragedies of life must be filed in the 'mystery' category in our minds. And that is especially true when we contemplate God's purpose for suffering in this fallen cosmos.

The book of Job is all about a righteous sufferer. But you cannot turn to Job to find the *answer* to suffering. In fact Job's 'comforters' were condemned by God for that very reason: Eliphaz, Bildad and Zophar tried to give neat-package solutions to Job's suffering that were so wide of the mark, they were offensive.

A profound mystery

And even when God appears on the scene at the end of the book, having silenced the 'empty words' of the comforters, he doesn't give Job a three-point sermon entitled 'What to do when you are suffering'. Instead God heightens the mystery by pointing to his mastery over all creation.

The God who tells the starry constellations where to shine and guides the path of the eagle's wing, is a God who views all the questions of life, including the purpose of suffering, from such a unique standpoint that we would not understand it even if he told us.

For some mysterious reason, the very suffering that God promises to banish in his new world, he nonetheless allows in this current creation and even uses for the benefit of his saints. Beyond that, there is no manual, no 'how to' for the mystery of suffering. The only thing more mysterious than suffering in our world is the God who allows it.

Don Carson has written a wonderful book entitled *How Long, O Lord?* That book is so helpful precisely because Carson does not offer a neat-package solution. Posing the title as a question says it all.

Suffering and the cross

However, while suffering is ultimately a mystery, I am not suggesting that God has nothing to say about it. He has a lot to say. And the most striking thing he has ever told us, he has said without even using words. Surely the naked man hanging in agony between two thieves under a darkened sky has something profound to say about the suffering that even the best Christians face in this bewildering world?

Much of this book so far has considered the results of Christ's suffering and what this has achieved for us. But there is also a message for us in the very suffering itself. The fact that God chose to procure our salvation through one of the most gruesome objects of human torture ever devised says something profound about God and suffering.

The Roman statesman Cicero famously wrote,

> It is a crime to put a Roman citizen in chains, it is an enormity to flog one, sheer murder to slay one; what, then, shall I say of crucifixion? It is impossible to find the word for such an abomination . . . let the very mention of the cross be far removed not only from a Roman citizen's body, but from his mind, his eyes, his ears.[1]

Our God is not a distant God who sits on a cloud totally removed from our pain. He is a God who squeezed full deity into a baby's frame, opened his soul to temptation, tiredness, hunger and tears, had the legitimacy of his birth questioned, was accused of being demon-possessed by religious leaders and a lunatic by his own family, was betrayed by the kiss of one of his closest friends, sentenced to death through a kangaroo court illegally cobbled together in the middle of the night, had his flesh torn open with a whip woven together with pieces of bone and metal (scourging), was mocked, spat upon and stripped of his clothing (crucified victims usually hung stark naked on their crosses). He was jeered through the streets of Jerusalem, perhaps by some of those he had healed, was laid on a crossbeam outside the city walls (a place of maximum ignominy), had Roman spikes smashed into his wrists until his nerve endings exploded, felt thorns digging into his delicate temples (a symbol of the futility of life in a sin-drenched creation), and all that before God 'laid on him the iniquity of us all' (Isaiah 53:6).

Christ's sufferings were not confined to the three hours of Calvary darkness. Hebrews suggests that his whole life was tinged with suffering, as he cried many tears to God, and in fact that 'he learned obedience through what he suffered' (Hebrews 5:8), which suggests a gradual process.

Isaiah simply calls Jesus 'a man of suffering', the kind of figure 'from whom people hide their faces' (Isaiah 53:3). Usually people have to hide their faces from God's glory. But at the cross they had to hide their faces from his shame.

> Man of sorrows! What a name
> For the Son of God, who came
> Ruined sinners to reclaim![2]

The God who suffers

Surely the cross says something profound about God's intimate involvement, his emotional connection with a world full of suffering. John Stott comments in his book

The Cross of Christ, about a visit he once made to a Buddhist temple:

I could never believe in God, if it were not for the cross . . .
In the real world of pain, how could one worship a God who
was immune to it? I have entered many Buddhist temples in
different Asian countries and stood respectfully before the
statue of Buddha, his legs crossed, arms folded, eyes closed,
the ghost of a smile playing round his mouth, a remote look
on his face, detached from the agonies of the world. But each
time after a while I have had to turn away. And in imagination
I have turned instead to that lonely, twisted, tortured figure on
the cross, nails through hands and feet, back lacerated, limbs
wrenched, brow bleeding from thorn-pricks, mouth dry and
intolerably thirsty, plunged in God-forsaken darkness. That is
the God for me! He laid aside his immunity to pain. He
entered our world of flesh and blood, tears and death. He
suffered for us. Our sufferings become more manageable in
light of his. There is still a question mark against human
suffering, but over it we boldly stamp another mark, the cross
which symbolizes divine suffering.[3]

What does the Gospel have to say to the majority of people
in the world who are poor and starving and needy, who are
unhappy and miserable and in pain? What we have got to
say to them is this, 'My God suffers like that; the cross is the
only place where any being has ever understood what you
are going through right now.'[4] *Donald English*

Comfort from the cross

Somehow a rich comfort emerges for every righteous sufferer
from the cross of Christ. Whatever questions lurk in our

minds as to why God allows suffering in our current creation, we know he is not a passive bystander.

Philippians 2 marvels not simply that Christ veiled his deity to become a man, or, greater mystery, that the immortal God should chose to die, but mystery of mysteries that it should be through death on a cross. Crucifixion was so horrid, as we saw earlier, that it was forbidden to crucify a Roman citizen, no matter how great his crime. A later Roman emperor, Constantine the Great (ironically the first emperor to proclaim himself a Christian) outlawed crucifixion as inappropriate for a civilized society.

So if you find yourself engulfed by suffering right now, or perhaps you have to watch someone you love going through the darkest tunnel of their lives, turn your eyes upon Jesus. If ever you need to look to Christ, it is now.

The necessity of suffering

So there is a deep comfort for us, as Christians struggling to come to terms with a sovereign, loving God on the one hand, and the suffering he allows on the other. That God entered our suffering in Christ is not so much an answer to that conundrum, but a balm for the soul.

But there is a still deeper mystery here. The New Testament view of suffering is not simply that Christ wants to assure us he understands what suffering is all about, because he has gone through it. The real mystery is that suffering is a vital part of our discipleship. To avoid it is to miss out on all that God wants us to be. Jesus actually invites us to join him in his suffering.

And this isn't a minor doctrine tucked away in the back-waters of Jude or Philemon. This is at the very heart of New Testament Christianity. As you read through the whole sweep of Acts, you cannot fail to see the connection between suffering and the growth of the church.

In Acts 5, Peter and the apostles are brought before the Sanhedrin for disobeying the command to keep quiet about Christ. Luke tells us they were 'flogged'. Howard Marshall says that this flogging 'was the Jewish punishment of "forty-lashes-minus-one" . . . It was no soft option; people were known to die from it'.[5]

For Peter, this was the first time he had received physical punishment for naming the name. But how did the apostles respond to being beaten black and blue? Luke adds, 'The apostles left the Sanhedrin, rejoicing because they had been counted worthy of suffering disgrace for the Name' (Acts 5:41).

> God takes us through afflictions in order to bring us to a recognition of our own helplessness, to bring our self confidence to an end, and to teach us an exclusive trust in God. In desperate times we learn to hold him fast.[6]
> *Jonathan Lamb*

Rejoicing in suffering?

The apostles saw suffering for Christ almost as a badge of honour, like an avid student working diligently to achieve a much-sought-after scholarship. 'They rejoiced that they had been counted worthy' to suffer. If we think this is some kind of strange masochism we find in the early days of the church, that was later tempered when the church began to mature, then we need to think again.

We find the same idea when Paul is teaching the Philippians. Paul is writing from prison, and has just given his triumphant 'for me to live is Christ, to die is gain' speech to these suffering Christians. Then he calls the believers to

conduct yourselves in a manner worthy of the gospel of Christ
. . . without being frightened in any way of those who oppose
you . . . For *it has been granted to you on behalf of Christ not only
to believe in him, but also to suffer for him, since you are going
through the struggle you saw I had, and now hear that I still have.*
(Philippians 1:27–30)

Suffering to Paul was not a sign that something had gone
tragically wrong with God's loving rule of the universe. Nor
was his attitude, 'Huddle together, holding tight to Jesus until
it is all over'. Nor did he suggest, as some prosperity teachers
might do, that suffering is a sign that you are lacking in faith.

Quite the opposite. For Paul, suffering was something
that God had graciously 'granted', on the same level of God
granting them belief in Jesus. Dare we say that suffering was a
gift? The same word that is behind the Greek word for 'granted'
is the word that is used in the New Testament to describe God
giving us his Son and God pouring out spiritual gifts on his
church: *charisma*, a word which implies a 'gift of grace'.

The fellowship of his sufferings

What a strange notion. That we should view suffering as
something that has been graciously granted to God's most
worthy servants. That we should rejoice to be found worthy
of suffering for Christ. Have you ever thought of your
suffering as a badge of honour? As something to rejoice in?

Why should we rejoice in suffering? Well, if you are familiar
with your New Testament, one stand-out passage comes
immediately to mind, doesn't it? 'Consider it pure joy, my
brothers and sisters, whenever you face trials of many kinds'
(James 1:2).

This is the bizarre idea that James opens his letter with. He
is barely through his tiny greeting sentence before launching

into this perplexing theme. But why on earth should we consider it joy when God grants it to us to suffer for him? 'Because you know that the testing of your faith develops perseverance. Let perseverance finish its work so that you may be mature and complete, not lacking anything' (James 1:3–4).

The crown-jewel of discipleship is what James calls Christian maturity. And a significant outpost on the road to maturity is perseverance. And the life experience that best produces perseverance is suffering. Suffering leads to perseverance, which leads to Christian maturity.

We need to be clear what James is *not* saying here. He is not saying that suffering *in itself* is something joyful. That is masochism, and masochism is a perverse notion: the joy of pain itself. When Christ was bent double in suffering, sweating drops of blood in Gethsemane, it would be perverse to suggest he was enjoying that experience.

Hebrews tells us it was 'for the joy set before him' that he '*endured* the cross' (Hebrews 12:2). Gethsemane to Golgotha was a road of agonizing endurance for Christ. What made him joyful was what his suffering would produce: that was the joy 'set before him'.

And in the same way, what gives us joy, says James, in the midst of our suffering, is the end result. It is the beauty of perseverance that leads to Christian maturity, developing a Christian character that is 'not lacking in anything'.

Can we learn to see suffering in this light? Not simply realizing that Jesus has suffered with us, but plunging deeper than that, to see Jesus inviting us to share in his nail-scarred hands? Could we perhaps have our deepest experiences of God and become mature through the refinement of suffering?

Paul produces some of his most insightful writing when he plunges into the mystery of Christian suffering in fellowship with Christ. Again to the Philippians, Paul says, 'I want to know

Christ – yes, to know the power of his resurrection and participation in his sufferings, becoming like him in his death' (3:10).

> We're nearly always longing for an easy religion, easy to
> understand, easy to follow, a religion with no mystery, no
> insoluble problems, no snags. A religion that would allow
> us to escape from our miserable human condition. A
> religion in which contact with God spares us all strife, all
> uncertainty, all suffering and all doubt. In short, a religion
> without a cross.[7] *George Hoffman*

The Wesley boys

I've been reading a lot recently about the life of John Wesley,
one of the most influential Christians in church history. But
it's fascinating to see the struggles, the suffering that John
Wesley faced, the different threads God knitted together to
give him this kind of perseverance in order to mature his faith.

John Wesley's father Samuel was a minister, but he was very
negligent of his family. He spent some time away on travels,
and was confronted by fellow ministers at one point for not
sending any cash from his clerical salary back to his family.

John Wesley was essentially raised in a single-parent home.
Not the ideal start for a passionate evangelist, you might think.
But an absentee father meant that John spent an unusual
amount of his childhood with his mother Susanna, who was
a most remarkable woman. Susanna Wesley had nineteen
children, but only ten of them survived into adulthood, two
of them being John and his brother Charles, who became the
great hymn writer.

But despite difficult home circumstances and a history of
grief in the family, Susanna faithfully set aside one night of the

week to talk to each of her ten children about their educational and spiritual development. She also taught them Hebrew and Greek. She was a model of the impact a godly mother can have on her children, even in the midst of adversity.

Another thread of suffering God wove into Wesley's childhood was a house fire. When he was just a small boy, the family home burned down, and he was narrowly rescued from the flames. His mother famously said he was 'a brand plucked from the burning'.

And that event in Wesley's life made him feel from his earliest days that he owed his whole life to God, and that God was going to do something special with him.

The 'Holy Club'

Wesley ended up at Oxford University, where he and his brother Charles met with an eighteen-year-old student called George Whitefield. The three of them together formed the 'Holy Club' in Oxford, where they read the New Testament together in Greek every week. They fasted every Wednesday and Friday, which quite often made all three of them ill. Friends and colleagues were concerned about how gaunt these zealous young men looked half the time.

That Holy Club was so despised by Oxford students that they used to throw rocks and mud at the three young men as they went for their sessions. But, according to their journals, it was actually having stones thrown at them that made the Wesleys and Whitefield so courageous.

John Wesley then developed a missionary zeal which took him to the US state of Georgia – no mean trip in the days before aeroplanes. But his mission trip was an absolute disaster, because all the Georgians hated Wesley for being so authoritarian and arrogant, just like his father before him had been. The whole trip was a humiliation for Wesley. And with his tail between his legs, he sailed home. But during the trip, the ship was caught up in a fearsome storm of Lake Galilee proportions.

The storm was so bad that Wesley was terrified and even feared losing his life. But he was amazed at the calm spirit that a group of Moravian Christians showed during this storm. The Moravians were a group of pietistic believers, known for their prayer life, led by their charismatic leader Nicolas von Zinzendorf. And these Moravians were the epitome of grace in the midst of the storm. Wesley, by contrast, was quaking in his boots. And Wesley's humiliation in Georgia, followed by his terror when faced with a storm at sea, troubled him so deeply, that he began to question whether he was in fact a believer at all.

That trouble and doubt eventually led him to a Moravian meeting back in London where someone was reading from Luther's commentary on the book of Romans. It came home to Wesley, for the first time in his life, that he could be saved by simple faith in Christ. As he wrote in his journal, 'I felt my heart strangely warmed.' His suffering actually led him to a deeper appreciation of the gospel of grace.

Persecuted preachers

From that point on, John Wesley and George Whitefield began preaching in churches in Oxford and Bristol with new zeal and a deep inner peace. But they were thrown out of the churches and banned from preaching because they were considered too zealous, too much of a threat to the sleepy Anglicanism of their era. And you could write a book about how Wesley and Whitefield, for the rest of their days, were frequently vilified and considered heretics by the establishment church, which denounced them publicly from the pulpit.

But it was because Wesley was banned from the churches that he decided to preach in the open fields alongside Whitefield, and ride around England on horseback, preaching the gospel wherever he went. And famously, for the next fifty years, Wesley travelled thousands of miles on horseback, preaching in open fields, often to crowds of fifty and sixty thousand, all around the country, changing the face of Britain. He introduced small groups of disciplined, accountable believers, who would become known as 'Methodists'. And the rest, as they say, is history.

But think about the threads of suffering that God drew together in Wesley's life to make him such a powerful Christian leader, to teach him the kind of perseverance that would lead to maturity. His father virtually abandoned him and his family. He nearly lost his life in a house fire as a child. He was pelted with mud and stones as he went to his Holy Club and he became ill through his early fasting experiences.

His humiliating mission tour to Georgia forced him to address his own arrogance. He nearly died in a storm at sea, which made him realize he had no peace with God. And he only started preaching around the country on horseback because he was banned from preaching in the established churches.

For all true Christian disciples, trials are extremely valuable. We share Christ's life, experiencing his suffering but also his resurrection life. We experience God's comfort as he draws alongside us by his Spirit. We help God's people as we share our suffering, our comfort and our prayers in the Christian family. And we trust God's purpose, which moves us away from self reliance, independence or even despair, so that we trust the God of the resurrection.[8] *Jonathan Lamb*

Suffering leads to maturity

I wonder what threads of suffering God is weaving together in your life at the moment to give you perseverance that leads to spiritual maturity? Will you allow the great physician to use his gracious scalpel on your soul?

Every Christian has two choices when they are thrown into a season of suffering. We can either blame God for taking us through a dark tunnel, when God should know better and cushion his children from the fire of trials. Or, we can accept the mysterious truth that pain, no matter how severe, can actually be a refining mechanism in our hearts, to teach us total dependence on Christ. We can ask Jesus, who knows all about suffering, to draw especially close, on the basis of Philippians 3, and allow us to know him in an altogether deeper way.

And if we are facing some kind of persecution for the sake of Christ's name, for the sake of the clear and courageous testimony we maintain for Jesus, can we get to the point where we emulate the apostles and say, 'I rejoice that I have been found worthy to suffer for the Name? I don't rejoice in the pain itself – it's horrible, Lord, and I despise the darkness of the pain every bit as much as Christ did in Gethsemane. But, Lord, you have taught me to rejoice that you only allow *redemptive* pain in the life of your children, the kind of pain that will lead to my maturing in Christ. Help me, Lord, to want to be mature as a saint of God, more than I want anything else in the world.'

If you can say that kind of prayer to the Lord, in the midst of the bleakness of your pain, it could well mean more to God than anything else you will do for him in this life. The moment when Jesus was offering the greatest act of worship in his whole life was the moment when he was facing his greatest agony on a cross. Worship in the midst of pain is actually the greatest achievement a human being can attain.

> When peace, like a river, attendeth my way,
> When sorrows, like sea billows, roll,
> Whatever my lot, Thou hast taught me to say,
> It is well, it is well, with my soul.[9]

Questions

1. What difference does 'Christ on a cross' make to your understanding of suffering?
2. How can suffering be a 'gift' from God?
3. Has this chapter changed your view on suffering? If so, how? If not, why not?

Passages for further study

Romans 8:18–39; Hebrews 11:36 – 12:13; 1 Peter 1:3–9.

9

The pilgrim's travel kit

Recently, I found myself reading a book on evolutionary theory. What struck me most about this book actually had nothing to do with evolution, but rather something quite unique about mankind, a trait in humanity that separates us from the animal world.

We love 'symbols'. And apparently that sets us apart as creatures. We can imagine, think in pictures, explore deeper meanings of reality, in a way that distinguishes us from any other creature. Our love of symbols, which we express in all the great works of art and poetry, literature and beauty, is part of what it means to be human – to be made 'in God's image'.

So it is no surprise that when Christ left the stage of history, he left us with two powerful symbols, so that the church could be constantly reminded of the power of the cross, pictures that encourage us to explore the deeper meaning of his cross, signs that allow us to participate in his cross today.

This chapter is an invitation to think again about those two great ordinances (some call them 'sacraments') of the church: baptism and communion. Surely it speaks of the centrality of the cross, that Jesus should leave us with two 'signs', encouraging every generation of believers to remember it.

Jesus did not ask us to remember his birth or commemorate any of his great miracles. But he did ask us to remember his death, and to do so regularly through bread and wine, and decisively through water baptism.

Baptism and communion picture for us 'cross-centred' discipleship. Baptism represents our initial immersion into the cross of Christ, and communion our ongoing commitment to Calvary.

Baptism: a picture of Christ's death

Let me say up front that I (Jeremy) come from a believers' baptism tradition, where we immerse rather than sprinkle. If you come from an infant baptism conviction, I hope this won't make you turn the page too quickly!

Baptism by immersion is the clearest way to express the radical death-burial-resurrection process which baptism symbolizes. Here is how Paul explains it in Romans:

> Don't you know that all of us who were baptized into Christ Jesus were baptized into his death? We were therefore buried with him through baptism into death in order that, just as Christ was raised from the dead through the glory of the Father, we too may live a new life.
> (Romans 6:3–4)

On one level, baptism is a re-enactment of the death, burial and resurrection of Christ himself. Lowering the believer under the water symbolizes Jesus' death and burial – the water is a kind of tomb – and raising him or her again, pictures the resurrection of Christ.

But baptism is more than a piece of theatre. It is a picture of what it means to be a Christian. When you are lowered into the water, you are identifying yourself with the death of Christ. You are saying in effect, 'I have died with Christ. My old way of living, where I worshipped my own desires and pursued my own agenda, is over now, as dead as a corpse in a tomb. That entire trajectory of life must be banished now from all my thinking, feeling and doing. I have died to myself. And I now rise to live a new life where Jesus' word and his glory become my soul-absorbing focus.'

A picture of cleansing

Alongside the picture of dying and rising again, baptism also symbolizes washing. When the apostle Paul met Christ on the road to Damascus, he was told to go and see Ananias. And the first thing Ananias encouraged this new convert to do was, 'Get up, be baptized and *wash your sins away*, calling on his name' (Acts 22:16).

The relationship between water and washing is clear. When we are baptized, we are declaring that we have participated in the saving effects of Christ's death. His death has washed away our sins. We are utterly clean in his sight, declared righteous by his grace, even though we remain sinners in practice.

It is important to emphasize that it is not the act of baptism that washes away our sins. As Paul makes clear in Galatians, there is no religious ritual – neither circumcision for the Jew nor baptism for the believer – that transfers any saving power to your life.

We are saved 'by grace alone, through faith alone, in Christ alone', as the sixteenth-century Reformers put it, not through any merit of our own, or any good work or religious observance we perform. We cannot add anything to Christ's finished work. Rather, baptism *symbolizes* what Christ has already done for us the moment we believed in him.

And what a beautifully simple picture baptism is of the deep cleansing Christ has accomplished in our hearts, through his death and resurrection. The song will be sung in the heavenly city,

> Unto Him who hath loved us and washed us from sin,
> Unto Him be the glory for ever. Amen.[1]
> (see Revelation 1:5–6)

A picture of passing through judgment

One of the least heralded, but most profound, pictures in baptism, is the idea of passing through the waters of God's judgment. Wayne Grudem's *Systematic Theology* points out how often water is used as a place of judgment in Scripture.

Noah's flood showed God judging the whole of mankind for their wickedness. The waters of the Red Sea were opened for Israel, but fell upon the approaching Egyptian army as a sign of judgment on the abusive superpower. And the book of Jonah finds the disobedient prophet cast overboard into the murky deep as a judgment for running away from his Nineveh assignment. Jonah chapter 2 is Jonah's psalm of repentance, as he sinks through various depths of water, which he clearly sees as a judgment from God, before the big fish rescues him by God's grace.

Baptism is a picture for the believer of passing through God's judgment, and coming out the other side. A little bit like Passover night in Egypt for the Israelites, the angel of death has 'passed over' us, not unleashing on us the judgment we deserve, because the blood of Christ is covering our hearts.

We have 'come out the other side' because of Jesus' resurrection. 'There is now no condemnation for those who are in Christ Jesus' (Romans 8:1).

> When Paul talks about baptism, he is not talking about some magical link-up with the past. Baptism is essentially an expression of faith and commitment in the present, and despite differing views about the mode of baptism, it is universally accepted among Christians as the initiatory ordinance or sacrament into the Body of Christ . . . We know that all the water can do is make you wet. Yet it is the outward visible sign of the inward, visible grace. And it is by that grace operating in our lives that we are initiated into the benefits and effects of Christ's death and resurrection.[2]
> *David Jackman*

Does your life reflect your baptism?

Am I living out my baptism? Or did I just tick the ceremony off my 'to do' list, without really thinking about the commitment to Christ it was symbolizing? It is easy for us to empty a symbol of its power and to denigrate the impact our baptism should have on our daily lives.

Have I really died to myself? It would be difficult to think of a more challenging picture. But dying to yourself is basic Christianity, not some goal for the spiritually elite when they have reached a certain peak of commitment to Christ.

People were baptized in the New Testament almost immediately following their conversion. On the day of Pentecost, about 3,000 people were baptized on the same day as Peter preached to them. Philip baptized many new converts in Samaria shortly after their conversion.

So baptism does not represent a deep moment of discipleship that a small percentage of Christians reach twenty or thirty years into their Christian commitment, while the rest of us dip our toes into more shallow streams. Baptism represents what Americans call 'Christianity 101', the absolute basics of Christian living. I must learn to die to my own selfish desires *from day one*. I am finished with 'me'. Christ now reigns as Master and Lord of every desire, ambition, thought and action.

Does your life reflect your baptism? Have you really participated in the death of Christ?

Easy believism

Easy believism is a deep concern, especially in Western churches today. A great deal of preaching focuses on 'the moment of conversion'. Our whole aim in preaching is to get people to say 'the sinner's prayer', as though saying a few words of repentance and 'asking Jesus into your life' represented the final word on salvation.

But words can be cheap, can't they? Jesus did not merely tell us that he loved us. He showed it to us with spikes in his head. Jesus did not leave us with a prayer to say, to 'seal the deal' on our salvation. Indeed, there is no example of a 'sinner's prayer' in the Bible. Instead, Jesus left us with a radical sign: baptism.

If we could put the meaning of baptism into the words of a prayer, it would not be, 'Lord Jesus, thank you for dying for me. Please forgive my sin, and come into my heart.'

It would be more like, 'Jesus, thank you for dying for me. Now help me to die. I realize how gut-wrenchingly awful and horrific every whiff of my sinful rebellion must be to your prefect character and white-hot glory. I want to put every self-centred thought in my head into a mortuary, and bury it down the deepest mine, by the power of your Spirit. No more gossip, no more jealousy and envy, no more empty materialism and lust for power, no more insisting on my own rights, wanting my own way with my spouse, my friends, my family or my boss. I have put an end to myself. Jesus, teach me to die an excruciatingly selfless death, and rise again to be someone who has "obedience to Jesus Christ" carved into my DNA.'

If that was our 'sinner's prayer', I wonder how many would come to the front during emotional evangelistic events to give their lives to Christ? Baptism cuts at the heart of 'easy believism'. As Paul said,

> I have been crucified with Christ and I no longer live, but
> Christ lives in me. The life I live in the body, I live by faith
> in the Son of God, who loved me and gave himself for me.
> (Galatians 2:20)

Baptized Christianity is summed up famously by Dietrich Bonhoeffer, 'When God calls a man, he bids him come and die.'

I wonder how many of us . . . are going to be led of the Holy Spirit to our own burial place, to give the honest consent of our hearts to the death of self. 'I am crucified with Christ.' If the cross does not mean that to you and to me it does not mean very much. That great big 'I'; that great personal pronoun, must be crossed out.[3] *Reginald Wallis*

Naked baptism

The early church took this idea of dying to oneself so literally that many of them were baptized naked. (In fact, that is why female deacons were introduced to many churches, not because the early church wanted gender equality, but because it was considered unseemly for a male elder or deacon to baptize a naked woman!)

Christians in the early church wanted to go as far as they could to symbolize this truth that 'when I gave my life to Christ, the old me had to be stripped away'. In Colossians, Paul talks about being 'buried with [Christ] in baptism' and 'raised with him' (2:12), and goes on to unpack this image of dying and rising again, taking off the old, and putting on the new:

> You died and your life is now hidden with Christ in God . . .
> Put to death whatever belongs to your earthly nature: sexual
> immorality, impurity, lust, evil desires and greed, which is
> idolatry . . . now you must also rid yourselves of such things
> as these: anger, rage, malice, slander, and filthy language from
> your lips. Do not lie to each other, since you have taken off your
> old self with its practices and have put on the new self, which is
> being renewed in knowledge in the image of its Creator.
> (Colossians 3:3–10)

Ouch! Naked baptism really hurts. But of course it's not simply about stripping away the 'old self'. There is a beautiful, Christ-shaped new self made available to us through the Spirit who takes permanent residence in our hearts.

> Therefore, as God's chosen people, holy and dearly loved,
> clothe yourselves with compassion, kindness, humility,
> gentleness and patience. Bear with each other and forgive
> one another if any of you has a grievance against someone.
> Forgive as the Lord forgave you. And over all these virtues
> put on love, which binds them all together in perfect unity.
> (Colossians 3:12–14)

Leave it all behind

A pastor from Texas was once visiting East Malaysia, where he attended a small church. The church happened to be conducting a baptism service that night. During the service, the pastor noticed some luggage leaning against the wall of the church building. He asked one of the elders about it.

The elder pointed to the girl who had just been baptized and told the pastor, 'Her father said that if she was baptized as a Christian, she could never go home again. So she brought her luggage.'

Thank God that not many of us have to be literally thrown out of our homes when we first confess Christ, but we are all called to leave things behind: old ways, old sins, old patterns of thinking that clash with following our crucified King.

Don't take the power out of the symbol. Baptism is not a one-off ceremony that we quickly leave behind. Baptism is the doorway to a whole new life. We have been immersed into the death of Christ. We carry our baptism with us, and its power should never leave us until the day we die.

We are people of the cross. And just as our Lord was stripped of his earthly clothing and had the skin torn from his back by whips, so we follow in his footsteps by taking off our old self, by being stripped of our fallen nature, however painful the process, and clothed anew in the righteousness of Jesus.

Baptism is not a quick bath at the front of church! It is a promise to God to strip ourselves naked of self-absorbed living, and immerse ourselves into the character of Jesus.

Are you keeping your promise?

Bread and wine

The cross is not only at the centre of the baptism ritual, but is the heartbeat of the other great ordinance Jesus left for every believer to observe. If baptism symbolizes our initial immersion into Christ, then communion keeps bringing us back to the cross, like a series of staging posts on our way to glory.

I was particularly taken by this entry in the August 2007 version of the daily devotional booklet *Our Daily Bread*:

> *Apollo 11* landed on the surface of the moon on Sunday, July 20, 1969. Most of us are familiar with astronaut Neil Armstrong's historic statement as he stepped onto the moon's surface: 'That's one small step for man; one giant leap for mankind.' But few know about the first meal eaten there.
>
> Buzz Aldrin had brought aboard the spacecraft a tiny Communion kit provided by his church. Aldrin sent a radio broadcast to Earth asking listeners to contemplate the events of that day and give thanks.
>
> Then, in radio blackout for privacy . . . [Aldrin] read, 'I am the vine, you are the branches. He who abides in me, and I in him, bears much fruit.'
>
> Silently, he gave thanks and partook.

The pilgrim's travel kit

I love this story of Buzz Aldrin plucking his communion travel kit out of his space suit as he looks down on planet Earth. It reminds me of an old hymn we used to sing:

> Shut in with thee, far, far above
> the restless world that wars below;[4]

Buzz Aldrin took those words literally as he broke bread 250,000 miles above the Earth! And this idea of a communion travel kit, a sacred meal we can share at any time, in any place, is helpful in understanding what communion is all about. Remembering the Lord's death regularly was one of the pillars on which church life was built, as part of its communal sharing of food.

> They devoted themselves to the apostles' teaching and to the fellowship, to *the breaking of bread* and to prayer . . . Every day they continued to meet in the temple courts. They *broke bread* in their homes with glad and sincere hearts. (Acts 2:42, 46)

Every time we come to this Table . . . our faith and our love operate in three ways: in relation to the past, this feast is a commemoration (of the darkness of Calvary); in relation to the present, it is a participation (in the salvation Christ has won for us); and in relation to the future, it is an anticipation (of the last great feast in glory).[5] *Francis W. Dixon*

The simplicity of communion

What seems to be emphasized here was the regularity with which the early church observed communion and the simplicity of the ceremony. They met each day in homes to break bread.

I remember standing in the church of St Peter's at the heart of the Vatican in Rome, watching a very ornate mass taking place. The archbishop was dressed in a flowing golden robe, choristers flanked him on either side, the smell of incense filled the air, all within a glorious cathedral whose very pillars took your breath away. It was all very ornate, but I was asking myself, 'Is this really what Jesus had in mind when he first instituted communion?'

I don't think so. Those first Christians remembered the Lord in their homes, perhaps with children sitting round on the floor. Remembering the cross of Christ was not some elaborate ceremony that demanded a sanctified officiator in flowing robes. That is not the New Testament picture at all.

When Jesus instituted the feast at the Last Supper, he was reclining in an upper room with his twelve best friends. Following his resurrection, he strolled along the road to Emmaus with two beleaguered disciples, and they broke bread, just the three of them, in a house in the early evening. And when the early church met for communion, they did it probably as part of the evening meal in their houses, just before sending the children to bed. Communion was to be a travel kit. Remembering the cross is not just for formal church services, but for when two or three are gathered on a Wednesday evening. Remembering the cross is something that should invade the daily normality of our lives. Christ's cross should be constantly before us.

And this thought of the informality and regularity of communion is reinforced by how normal and everyday the elements are. Jesus did not tell us to remember his death with caviar and champagne, but with bread and wine.

Wine was the everyday 'juice' of Jewish meal times. And the bread that Christ first broke would have been the unleavened variety that looked more like a cream cracker. These were everyday symbols found on even the poorest Jewish meal table. And that was the whole point.

Everything about communion points to a very simple ceremony that was to be repeated in everyday household scenarios, to encourage Christians to remember the cross *all the time* – not just three times a year on especially holy weekends.

My co-pastor in Aberdeen told me recently that missionary colleagues of his were visiting him from Naples. They enjoyed a great weekend together, and on the Sunday evening at home, before the friends were about to depart the next day, they took out a bread bun and some grape juice, and remembered the cross.

So often our ornate ceremonies distance us from the passion behind communion. One of the great breakthroughs of the Protestant Reformation was that the scriptures came into people's homes. They stopped being the reserve of ordained clergy who presided over mass in Latin, a language the rank and file could not understand.

John Wycliffe's famous dream was that a twelve-year-old ploughing a field would be able to enjoy the Scriptures. And I believe we need a similar reformation in communion today, which has in some cases become too ornate – hidden behind flowing robes and golden goblets. Communion is for the everyday people of God.

The meaning of communion

As we break the bread, we remember Christ's body, totally given for us. As we sip the wine, we celebrate his blood poured out for our sins. In this way, we re-enact Calvary, just as we do in the baptism ceremony: 'Whenever you eat this bread and drink this cup, you *proclaim* the Lord's death until he comes' (1 Corinthains 11:26).

But again, it's not just theatre. When I physically take the bread and wine to my lips, I am reminded that I have participated in the death of my Lord. Hear the invitation of Jesus to 'take and eat; this is my body' (Matthew 26:26). I am invited, as a guest of the Lord, to enjoy the benefits of this glorious salvation that is saving me every moment of every day.

Just as bread and wine nourish and strengthen my body, so the death of Christ nourishes and strengthens my soul. That's the meaning behind Jesus' strange words: 'My flesh is real food and my blood is real drink. Whoever eats my flesh and drinks my blood remains in me, and I in them' (John 6:55–56).

There is nothing that strengthens and revitalizes my whole Christian experience more than reminding myself that he died for me. My sins are gone, as far as East from West (Psalm 103:12). Jesus loves me. This salvation is for me, and God planned to adopt me as his child before the world began.

John Duncan used to be Professor of Hebrew at Edinburgh University. He was sitting one day at communion in a church in the Highlands of Scotland, and he was feeling so personally unworthy that when the elements came round, he felt he couldn't take them, so he allowed the bread and wine to pass.

As he was sitting there feeling absolutely miserable, he noticed a girl in the congregation who, when the bread and wine came round, also allowed them to pass, and then broke down into tears. That sight seemed to bring back to the ageing Bible scholar the truth he had forgotten. And in a carrying whisper that floated across the church, he was heard to say, 'Take it, lassie, take it. It's meant for sinners.' And he himself did just that.

What encouragement there is, especially when our hearts are heavy because we have failed the Lord in some way, to come back to bread and wine, and remember the forgiveness and welcome that flow to sinners from the broken body and poured-out blood of Christ.

> The spiritual banquet is coming. There's so much in the Bible about feasting. We're all headed for a great feast. The richest of fare (Isaiah 55) is simply an anticipation of an eschatological [end-times] feast in which the food will be sumptuous beyond our wildest dreams. The Marriage Supper of the Lamb is coming. Feast now on him and enjoy the richest of fare and anticipate that day when, with every saint from every nation, we will dine at the heavenly table, feasting forever with him.[6] *Steve Gaukroger*

The marriage supper of the Lamb

Eating and drinking with God is an image we find throughout Scripture of deep fellowship with the Lord. Adam and Eve before the fall ate the fruit God had provided in his presence, before being cast out – an angel's flashing sword preventing them from eating from God's garden ever again.

But at Mount Sinai, God invited Moses and the elders of Israel up the mountain to eat and drink in his presence, and he instituted a series of sacred feasts in Israel's calendar where they could eat and drink in the presence of the Lord once again: Passover, Tabernacles, Pentecost and so on.

But those feasts of the Old Covenant are not as rich as the Lord's Supper, where the gathered church, redeemed by Christ's blood, meets to take bread and wine in anticipation of the feast we will enjoy in glory – the marriage supper of the Lamb. With glorified bodies and souls, and sin forever banished from human experience, we will eat and drink in the unhindered presence of the risen Lord: 'Then the angel said to me, "Write this: Blessed are those who are invited to the wedding supper of the lamb!" ' (Revelation 19:9).

Every time we take bread and wine, we are anticipating that future feast in a renewed creation. We only eat and drink 'until he comes'.

Questions

1. How would you explain the meaning of baptism to a non-Christian friend?
2. Are you living out your baptism?
3. Why is the simplicity of communion so central to its meaning?

Passages for further study

Romans 6:1–14; 1 Corinthians 11:17–32; Colossians 3:1–17.

Part four:
The resurrection factor

10

'If Christ has not been raised . . .'

The renowned English atheist Christopher Hitchens, who has very eloquently debated evangelicals all over the world, is not known for his sound theology. He is author of the subtly-entitled *God Is Not Great: Why Religion Poisons Everything*.

But Hitchens stepped outside the evangelical camp recently to debate with a thoroughly liberal, Unitarian minister called Marilyn Sewell. And during the debate, Hitchens defined quite beautifully what a Christian believes, much to the displeasure of his liberal opponent. The following exchange took place near the start of the interview:

Sewell: The religion you cite in your book is generally the fundamentalist faith of various kinds. I'm a liberal Christian, and I don't take the stories from the Scripture literally. I don't believe in the doctrine of atonement (that Jesus died for our sins, for example). Do you make any distinction between fundamentalist faith and liberal religion?

Hitchens: I would say that if you don't believe that Jesus of Nazareth was the Christ and Messiah, *and that he rose again from the dead* and by his sacrifice our sins are forgiven, you're really not in any meaningful sense a Christian.[1]

Sewell was hugely embarrassed, fumbled about with her notes for a moment, and then blurted out, 'Let me go someplace else.'

The crucial importance of the resurrection

It is a strange reality that many books dealing with the cross spend little or no time discussing the crucial importance of the resurrection. Quite simply, if Jesus Christ did not rise from the dead, his death on the cross was powerless and meaningless. There is no Christianity without the resurrection.

The resurrection of Jesus is not an event to be kept separate from his death for our sins. His death, burial, resurrection and exaltation form one single, sweeping salvation event. Take away or minimize any part of that salvation sweep and you end up with no gospel at all. That is how serious the issue of resurrection is to the meaning of Christian salvation.

But can Christians be confident that a miraculous event like a resurrection really did happen? Can we defend such an improbable event in the face of the many sceptics all around us? I think we can. Indeed I think we *must*, not simply because the gospel depends on it, but because there is a considerable amount of credible evidence that forces us to take such an unlikely an event as Christ's resurrection very seriously.

From Old Testament prophecies to New Testament preaching, and judging by the confidence with which the early apostles declared the resurrection, there is firm ground on which we can take our stand.

Old Testament prophecies

The witness of the Old Testament prophets to the resurrection of Messiah is often underestimated. Psalm 16 is considered a messianic Psalm, in which David says, 'You will not let your faithful one see decay.'

Isaiah 53 demands some kind of resurrection. This great 'servant song' speaks about the Messiah dying for the sins of Israel, then adds, 'He was assigned a grave with the wicked, and with the rich in his death' (Isaiah 53:9). This is a clear reference pointing to the wealthy Joseph of Arimathea placing Christ's corpse in his newly-hewn tomb. But following his death and burial

> He will see his offspring and prolong his days,
>   and the will of the LORD will prosper in his hand.
> After he has suffered
>   *he will see the light of life and be satisfied . . .*
> Therefore I will give him a portion among the great,
>   and he will divide the spoils with the strong,
> because he poured out his life unto death.
> (Isaiah 53:10–12)

The clear implication is that the servant who 'was pierced for our transgressions' would die, be buried in a wealthy man's tomb and would rise again to 'see the light of life'. A dead servant, so humiliated in death, who remains in his grave, could hardly be the triumphant Saviour who would 'see his offspring' (all those who believe in him), without a bodily resurrection.

Jesus himself highlights Psalm 110, another messianic psalm, where God invites the future Messiah (whom David calls 'lord') to come and sit at his right hand:

The LORD said to my lord,
  'Sit at my right hand,
until I make your enemies
  a footstool for your feet.'
(Psalm 110:1)

This is the most quoted psalm in the New Testament, because it points so clearly to both the deity of Jesus (David's 'lord'), his ascension into heaven ('sit at my right hand'), and the future full consummation of his reign, where God will bring all Christ's enemies under his rule. None of these promises could be fulfilled unless Christ had risen from the dead and taken up his rightful place at the right hand of God in glory.

The sweep of Old Testament prophecy

But it's not so much any one prophecy or Old Testament verse that predicts the resurrection. It's the full sweep of Old Testament promise pointing to the Messiah that demands a resurrection. Two key images of who the Messiah would be emerge.

One had to do with suffering, as in the servant of Isaiah 53, but also in Zechariah's prophecies: 'Strike the shepherd and the sheep will be scattered', 'They will look upon me, the one they have pierced' (Zechariah 13:7; 12:10). Isaiah and Zechariah clearly point to a suffering, dying Messiah.

But the Jews were carried away with the image of Messiah as king, a king to whom all the nations would come in order to seek teaching and counsel (Isaiah 2:1–5). In addition to Psalm 110, there is a whole series of coronation psalms that depict the Messiah taking his throne and ruling over the nations.

So you are left with two seemingly contradictory pictures: a suffering, dying Messiah who would be despised and rejected, and a conquering king Messiah who would rule over the nations and sit at God's right hand until God crushed his enemies under his feet.

And the resurrection is the 'bridge' that brings the two images together. Christ would come into our world first of all as the man of sorrows whose destiny was a cross where he would be 'wounded for our transgressions'. But, through his resurrection, God would defeat the powers of sin and death, and exalt his Son to the highest place. He is seated at God's right hand today, having accomplished the work of redemption. His resurrection means that sin, death, Satan and hell are defeated. And the resurrected, victorious Christ now waits in heaven until God has subdued all his enemies.

And one day he will come back as conquering King to take his crown, and the nations will be drawn to him in worship. The image of suffering servant and conquering king are brought together by the resurrection of Christ from the dead.

How many of the Old Testament prophets understood that God would visit us in this spectacular way in which there would first be suffering, shame, pain, the cross; followed by vindication, glory, triumph, life? They could see some elements but they didn't have it all together. They wanted to, they searched intently and with the greatest care, we are told . . . [but] the Christians see these things, because we live this side of their fulfilment, in one who is simultaneously God and man, in one who is simultaneously suffering servant and triumphant king, who was simultaneously the sacrificial lamb and the triumphant promised Messiah.[2] *D. A. Carson*

New Testament preaching

When we come to the New Testament, it is fascinating to note the kind of preaching the apostles engaged in as the early church began to blossom in the book of Acts. What was their message? Acts is built around nine 'sermons', mostly from Peter and Paul, as Luke educates us about the content of true gospel preaching.

It will not surprise you to know that Christ's death on the cross is mentioned in eight of these nine sermons. But do we need to be told that Christ's resurrection is mentioned in all nine? The apostles rushed out onto the streets of Jerusalem, preaching the resurrection of Jesus Christ as the definitive, world-changing sign that God had accepted Christ's sacrifice for sin and the powers of death and hell were vanquished forever.

The resurrection was at the heart of the apostles' message. They would not even have begun preaching at all if it had not been for the resurrection. The resurrection lit the fuse of gospel proclamation.

Jesus died on the cross for the sin of the whole world, in order to deal with the judgement of your sin. He was raised from the dead with power to impart this resurrection life to you. Do you believe that Christ went to death for your sin? Do you believe that life divine is his risen and ascended gift to you? Not only for others, not an official dogma, not a philosophical concept, but precious life, resurrection life from him to you! If thou believest so, thou art justified before God.[3] *Theo M. Bamber*

The apostles began preaching about an empty tomb (which neither the Jews nor the Romans could deny) within days of the resurrection, in the very city where the tomb could easily be found.

The resurrection is the only event that could account for the change of heart in the disciples, from disillusioned mourners to daring missionaries who were prepared to be martyred for their cause. Many people in history have died for a lie, but very few have died for what they *knew* to be a lie – a massive cover-up of their own making. When you read the Gospels, do you get the sense that these men are deliberate liars?

By their own admission, the disciples were left utterly distraught by the death of Christ. They were meeting in fear behind closed doors, hoping that the same Jewish leaders who had crucified their Lord would not be after them next.

What turned these ordinary men into fearsome preachers who left their quiet Galilean lives to blaze a trail for Christ across the ancient world?

Galilean realism

Galilean fishermen are realists. Like modern-day Yorkshiremen, they 'call a spade a spade'; they do not suffer from delusions of grandeur. So what led a fisherman like Peter, known for his often clumsy realism, to leave his fishing village of Capernaum to spread the message of Jesus far and wide, ending up as a crucified martyr thirty years later, 3,000 miles away from his birthplace, in Rome, under Emperor Nero?

What made the coward at Jesus' trial run like a maniac into the streets of Jerusalem, proclaiming that Jesus was the Son of God (Acts 2)? What made him tell a vast assembly of more than 3,000 Jews, who could have assaulted him, that they had murdered the Messiah? Where did this new-found courage come from?

And how did these first Christians get people from all walks of life, in very different parts of the world, to believe the incredible story that a crucified Jewish carpenter was the Son of God? And yet believe it they did! Right across Asia and Europe, into Rome itself, people came to believe in the resurrection of Jesus of Nazareth.

History records that everyone from slaves and housewives to former Jewish priests and wealthy patrons, to members of Caesar's own household, believed this crazy message!

Why? Because the apostles' testimony to the resurrection of Christ was so compelling. It had the ring of truth about it, and the Holy Spirit took that truth and fired it into the souls of people from 'every tribe, tongue, nation and language'. And all their hearers could see that these ordinary men and women were prepared to die for their belief in the resurrection.

> [We cannot] know the power of the risen Christ while at the same time doubting or denying the fact of the resurrection. Everywhere in the New Testament the exposition is joined to the event . . . there are those who talk about knowing the power of the risen Christ, while saying also that the resurrection is not exactly a fact of history . . . If the event never happened, then the spiritual truth that is built upon the event, and rises out of it, is all in vain, and of no significance.[4] *H. W. Cragg*

An early creed

What is so amazing about the birth of Christianity is that the whole church, from extremely early on, believed in a creed which had the resurrection as its heartbeat. Earlier (in chapter two) we considered 1 Corinthians 15:3, which tells us 'Christ died for our sins'. The vast majority of scholars believe this to be part of a creed that was passed down to Paul from the apostles:

that Christ died for our sins . . .
that he was buried,
that he rose again on the third day according to the Scriptures,
and *that* he appeared to Cephas, and then to the Twelve.

Paul is not inventing this creed. It had already been well established among the apostles. The repetition of the word 'that' shows us that Paul is repeating, word for word, this handed-down tradition.

Paul was writing to Corinth within fifteen years of Christ's death. So this Christian creed, which was given to him, must have been put together and agreed by the whole church even earlier than that. In fact we can work out when it was given to Paul, because he actually tells us. In Galatians 1:18–19 Paul says that he went to visit Peter and James, the key apostles, three years after Paul himself was converted. That is no more than five years after the crucifixion, and this creed was already established in the church.

This is really important because many liberal scholars believe that no-one considered Jesus as God before Paul came along, and that Paul invented Christianity by turning the human Jesus into a god, when there was no evidence for that.

That is clearly nonsense, if all the early Christians had already accepted the creed that Jesus had risen from the dead, and were preaching the resurrection publicly. The first Christians had a very high 'Christology' (view of Christ) very early on, because they believed so firmly in the resurrection of the Son of God.

A united church

And what is so fascinating about this creed is that the church united around it. All the early Christians knew there was no Christianity without the resurrection. And they all believed the incredible truth that Jesus of Nazareth had risen from the dead.

How did they achieve such unity, based on a miracle? The early church argued with one another about many things. Acts paints a very unflattering picture of the church arguing about food distribution among the widows (Acts 6). They argued very heatedly about the inclusion of Gentiles in the church (Acts 15). So heated was this debate that all the key leaders of the church had to come together for what became known as the Jerusalem Council, and a compromise decision had to be reached to appease both Jewish traditionalists and Gentile newcomers.

Paul and Barnabas themselves had an infamous clash over whether Barnabas' cousin, John Mark, should be allowed to go on mission with them, because he had deserted them on their first journey. Acts portrays the arguments of the early church 'warts and all'.

And yet the church is utterly united from its earliest days about the most difficult truth of all to believe – that Jesus had risen from the grave. There are no disputes about that. There are no awkward bust-ups or church divisions or major church councils.

How do you achieve unity about such a miraculous event that then becomes the cornerstone around which the whole church community unites?

An invented resurrection?

Leading Bible scholar Tom Wright argues brilliantly that the very concept of resurrection was so alien to the ancient world that none of the disciples could possibly have invented it. No one believed in bodily resurrections in that age. No other religions were based on resurrections.

Some strict Jews believed that there would be a final resurrection at the end of time, but even that was debated at the heart of Judaism between Pharisees and Sadducees. No Jew was expecting even a *crucified* Messiah, much less a *resurrected* one!

When Jesus told his disciples he was going to die, Peter took him aside to rebuke him for such silly talk (Mark 8:32). And when Jesus told them repeatedly he would rise from the dead, they had disputes with one another about what resurrection even meant (Mark 9:10). In light of this, a bodily resurrection was not something the disciples were ever likely to invent. Even when the women reported the empty tomb, the men did not believe them (Luke 24:22–24) and remained in a room 'with doors locked for fear of the Jews' (John 20:19).

It seems highly unlikely that the disciples would have happened to work the resurrection into a sophisticated, coherent theology overnight (which would accord with very subtle Old Testament prophecies), become martyrs for preaching it around the world and manage to convince millions in the process about this cornerstone of the faith, if Christ had not truly risen.

If the resurrection had been an invented con trick, then surely the theological weight placed on it would have cracked at some stage? But no. The bodily resurrection of Jesus Christ from the dead has stood the test of time, and remains a central tenet of the faith two thousand years later.

Confidence in the resurrection

So why are we so quiet about the resurrection? Why are we happy to talk about the cross, but reticent to declare the truth of the resurrection? Perhaps it's because we secretly feel we are opening up a can of worms which will lead any reasonable person to reject our gospel.

In a day when science seems to be god, and men like Richard Dawkins scoff at the claim of Christian miracles, some Christians, even ministers, prefer to keep quiet about the resurrection, perhaps because of embarrassment.

But there is no need to keep quiet. We actually need to follow in the apostles' footsteps and invite people to investigate the claims behind the resurrection, in the firm confidence that our faith is built on solid foundations.

Paul went to the very heartland of sceptical philosophers, the city of Athens (Acts 17), the place where the likes of the Richard Dawkins of their day used to congregate, scratching their beards, and throwing their PhDs at any supernatural hysteria among them.

And what did Paul preach? How did he ease his way into the hearts of the sceptics? By going for the jugular of course! Here is the crescendo of his message '[God] has set a day when he will judge the world with justice by the man he has appointed. He has given proof to this to everyone by raising him from the dead' (Acts 17:31).

Don't retreat when the resurrection is questioned

Paul's mention of the resurrection caused such consternation that he had to stop speaking. The great apostle worked hard at using language people could understand, and making the Christian faith sound as reasonable and accessible as possible in every different culture to which he preached. That's one of the central messages of Acts: adapting the message to your audience.

So it is all the more noteworthy that Paul does not try and cover up or soft-pedal the 'difficult' truth of the resurrection to cynical sceptics, despite knowing that many would scoff.

The way they responded in Athens was symptomatic of the way pagans everywhere respond to the preaching of the resurrection: 'When they heard about the resurrection of the dead, some of them sneered, but others said, "We want to hear you again on this subject"' (Acts 17:32).

Isn't that the kind of response we should expect every time we talk about our 'scandalous' gospel? Some sneer, but some will want to hear more. Or as Paul put it, to some we are 'an aroma that brings death', but to others 'an aroma that brings life' (2 Corinthians 2:16).

Paul did not hold back, retreat into his shell or get nervous about his bold pronouncements. The convinced apostle even faces up squarely to the implications of the resurrection story being false.

He tells us, with disarming boldness, that 'if Christ has not been raised, your faith is futile; you are still in your sins' (1 Corinthians 15:17). This is astonishingly bold and risky. If Jesus has not risen, would the last person out of church please switch off the lights? Close down your great cathedrals, blow out your candles, tear up your creeds and de-saint all your martyrs. The whole Christian enterprise is finished, the Bible is irrelevant and life is meaningless if Jesus Christ did not conquer death.

Is Paul really suggesting that the whole truth of the Christian faith rests on a miracle which so many philosophers and historians have sought to discredit over the centuries? Yes, that's exactly it. He goes as far as to say that his whole life as a preacher is a sad joke – what Shakespeare would call, 'a tale told by an idiot, full of sound and fury, signifying nothing' – if Christ has not risen:

> If Christ has not been raised, our preaching is useless and so
> is your faith. More than that, we are then found to be false

witnesses about God, for we have testified about God that he raised Christ from the dead.

(1 Corinthians 15:14–15)

Here is the New Testament's most prominent spokesman telling us, without blinking, that he is a liar, his life is a joke, and the whole of Christianity is without foundation, if there is no empty tomb.

Be bold about the resurrection

Paul and his fellow apostles' preaching tells me two things. First, the resurrection is crucial to the whole of Christian theology, and second, the early apostles were extremely confident that the resurrection was historical fact.

It is Paul's very boldness which is so attractive. He is not trying to hide the fact that his whole life and faith are based on whether or not this incredible miracle occurred. Rather, he is bold about the centrality of the resurrection, just as he was in Athens, just as all the apostles were as they preached the gospel across Asia and Europe in the first century, setting the standard for succeeding generations of gospel preachers.

And Paul has hard facts to back up his confidence. He speaks about more than five hundred believers who saw the risen Lord, not in a one-off hallucination, but in a huge variety of settings: in rooms, on a beach, on top of a mountain. He spoke to them, ate with them and taught them 'many things'.

The fact that 1 Corinthians is considered by the majority of scholars to be an 'early' letter is doubly impressive. Paul is almost inviting his readers to look up the names and addresses of some of the individuals who had seen the risen Christ, *because they were still alive when he was writing.*

A very public letter like 1 Corinthians would not have gained the prominence it did, if the incredible facts Paul outlines could have been easily dismissed. The more you investigate the incredible claims of the first Christians, the more you conclude that the resurrection of Christ was indeed a real event.

Old Testament prophecies point to it; New Testament preaching is centred round it; the church's creeds are based on it; and eyewitness evidence exists of the many who actually saw Christ risen and had their lives transformed.

> We do not look to the cross alone: we look to an empty tomb. And we do not look to an empty tomb that never had a cross before it. The cross and the empty tomb are together one great mighty act of God.[5] *H. W. Cragg*

Proclaim the resurrection

The German theologian Wolfhart Pannenberg wrote,

> The evidence for Jesus' resurrection is so strong that nobody would question it except for two things: First, it is a very unusual event. And second, if you believe it happened, you have to change the way you live.[6]

We need to follow in Paul's footsteps among the sceptical Athenians, boldly proclaiming the resurrection of Jesus Christ. We need to invite our neighbours, friends and thinking sceptics to evaluate the evidence themselves; the evidence, not just of history or prophecy, but that of changed lives.

When Paul first met the risen Jesus on the road to Damascus, everything changed. The religious terrorist became such a passionate preacher that he was prepared to lose his life for

Christ. When the two disciples on the road to Emmaus, heads down and souls battered by the crucifixion, realized that the stranger breaking bread with them was the risen Christ, everything changed. Before they realized it was Jesus, they had declared that it was too dark to travel. But when their eyes were opened to Jesus, the danger became secondary, and they raced back the seven-mile trip to Jerusalem, to report their excitement to the other disciples (see Luke 24:13–35).

What will it take for everything to change in your life? The best advert for a resurrected Christ is a bold, Christ-centred, witnessing believer. The story is told of when renowned atheist David Hume was scolded by some of his friends because he went to church each Sunday to hear the orthodox Scottish minister John Brown. Hume defended himself and replied, 'Well, I don't believe all that he says, but he does, and once a week I like to hear a man who believes what he says.'

What a difference it makes when convicted Christians are willing to talk about, and boldly defend, the truth of the resurrection with burning hearts and excitement in their voices, because Jesus means the world to them. Even atheists will be drawn to listen to those whose hearts are on fire for Christ.

Be an advert for the resurrection!

So why not become an advert for Christ's resurrection? If you are anything like us, you will be so used to hearing that 'Christ died for our sins and rose again on the third day' that the immensity of that truth has become dulled over time.

But when the Spirit reminds you that death died the day Jesus died, that his resurrection is a promise of our future resurrection, and that the empty tomb shines a sparkling hope into the hopelessness and futility of today's secularism, then you cannot keep that secret to yourself.

If we could just recapture the excitement that drove the Emmaus disciples back to Jerusalem, that gave wings to Paul's feet as he took the gospel across Asia and Europe, and that inspired the apostles to run like mad men into the streets of Jerusalem on the day of Pentecost to proclaim the resurrection, then revival might return to our lost and cynical nation.

Changed lives are the best proof of Jesus' resurrection. The British author A. N. Wilson became known for his scathing public attacks on Christianity, after his 'conversion' to atheism. But at Easter 2009, he amazingly returned to the faith, celebrating Easter at his local church. He commented in a *Daily Mail* article,

> My own return to faith has surprised none more than myself . . . My belief has come about in large measure *because of the lives and examples of people I have known* – not the famous, not saints, but friends and relations who have lived, and faced death, in light of the resurrection story, or in the quiet acceptance that they have a future after they die.[7]

Are you an advert for the resurrection? Would you like to become one? If you do, then ask the Spirit to re-infuse you with the same conviction that made Paul pen the words, 'But Christ has indeed been raised from the dead, the firstfruits of those who have fallen asleep' (1 Corinthians 15:20). And then go out and tell someone – today!

Questions

1. Why is it crucial for Christians to believe in the literal, bodily resurrection of Christ? How would it change Christianity if Christ had not literally risen?

2. Why do you think some Christians are reticent to talk about the resurrection? Why is it important to include the resurrection when we share the gospel?

Passages for further study

Luke 24:1–35; 1 Corinthians 15:1-11; 1 Peter 1:3–12.

11

The hope of glory

Lee Eclov, a Pastor from Chicago, tells the following moving story about a member of his congregation whom he visited – a man who was soon to die of cancer.

On the afternoon of May 2, 1990, I heard holy things. I was visiting Larry Hildreth, a father and husband from our church in Pennsylvania. He was in his thirties, but he was near death. I was at his home to serve him Communion, because he was too weak to come to church.

Larry was a deeply thoughtful man, and as he spoke that day, slow and deliberately, I realized I was hearing extraordinary things. I started scribbling them down on the margins of a bulletin in my Bible.

'Even if I have a short time to live,' Larry said, 'God has given me a great hope. Sometimes life throws us some tremendous curves, but death has lost its sting.'

In his struggle with cancer, it was clear that Larry had learned a lot about weakness. 'At the point in my life when I'm the weakest,' he said, 'I'm the strongest I've ever been.'

We started talking about his funeral, which as it turned out, would be exactly one month later. He told me he wanted lots of singing. (I remember how in church Larry would put his head back and sing with such unabashed gusto.) He said, 'The only thing I want people to think on that day is joy.' As he said this, he raised his hands to offer a slow, triumphant clap. 'When I pass into his kingdom, I envision this spectacular light – this spectacular feeling of being able to let go,' he said. 'I've felt a lot of grief for my children, my wife, my family, myself. But I've had to get over that. And once you get past that, you know that God is there, [and there's] that spirit of joyfulness. It's going to be a happy day for me. No grief for me.'[1]

Resurrection power

We've seen the facts behind the resurrection and the confidence we can have as Christians today that the cornerstone of our faith is secure. We can declare the resurrection boldly, without embarrassment, and let the Holy Spirit do his own convincing.

But the resurrection is more than a fact with consequences for today. It's a promise of future glory. That is why a believer like Larry Hildreth can dare to speak of 'joy' when he draws his last breath, of passing into the kingdom, of a spectacular light, and a risen, triumphant, loving Christ ready to greet him with open arms.

That is the hope for every believer. And in 1 Corinthians 15, the great resurrection chapter, Paul goes into glorious detail about this hope. He describes Jesus' resurrection as the 'firstfruits' of our resurrection. The firstfruits were the first takings of the crop at harvest time, with the promise that there was so much more to follow. And Paul continues, 'For as in Adam all die, so in Christ all will be made alive. But each in turn: Christ, the firstfruits; then, when he comes, those who belong to him' (1 Corinthians 15:22–23).

I can't think of a more exciting verse in the whole Bible. We all died 'in Adam', meaning that we were born facing the same separation from God that our ancestor faced when he ate the forbidden fruit. But just as Adam's condemnation was 'handed down' to us, so the power of Christ's resurrection is also handed down to all who believe in him. That means not only are we filled with the life of God here and now, but Christ's resurrection guarantees that one day we will rise again from the dead, just as Christ did. And we will rise to an altogether higher plane of living.

The second half of 1 Corinthians 15 describes the power of this new resurrection life.

From frailty to glory

Paul voices the question of a sceptic: 'How are the dead raised? With what kind of body will they come?' (1 Corinthians 15:35). The tone is, 'Come on Paul, be serious. When a body dies and is placed in the grave, it's powerless and decayed. How can you say that the dead are raised?' And of course many people today have exactly the same problem with the whole idea of resurrection. When we die, they put us in the ground and that's it. There's no more to be said.

But notice how confidently Paul replies. 'You fool', is the literal Greek. Paul insists that we see this kind of amazing resurrection happening all around us. If you look at the natural world, death and resurrection are at the heart of the cosmos and 'what you sow does not come to life until it dies'.

Think about the everyday miracle of the seed that we put in the ground. A seed is dry and dull, seemingly lifeless. If you looked at the seed itself, you wouldn't believe it had the capacity for greatness. But when you put it in the ground, God gives it miraculous power, and that dry, seemingly barren seed suddenly springs into a beautiful, vigorous flower. The seed is totally transformed into something much greater and more glorious.

Now how does that happen? says Paul. It's miraculous and yet it's happening all the time. And if God has the power to transform that dull little seed into a flower that is vigorous and beautiful and much grander than the seed, then why can't he do that with human bodies?

Just like the seed, our bodies when they die look fragile and decayed when buried in the ground. But God will transform the dead bodies of believers into glorious, vigorous new bodies at the resurrection.

You will have a heavenly body!

Then Paul takes this illustration of the natural world even further. He says, look at all the different *kinds* of bodies God has already created, each one suited to its own environment. There are bodies that are fitted for the earth: 'People have one kind of flesh, animals have another, birds another and fish another' (verse 39).

But there are also bodies that hang in the heavens above us. They are of a different order altogether, belonging in outer space, beyond the structures of the earth. And each one has their own kind of glory: 'The sun has one kind of splendour, the moon another and the stars another' (verse 41).

So if God is able to make bodies that suit the earth and a whole different order of bodies that belong in the heavens, then is he not able to take these frail earthly bodies and transform them into glorious bodies that are fit for a heavenly existence? Fit for eternity? Fit for the world of spirits and angels and the intimate presence of God himself?

There's wonderful encouragement in these verses for aging believers. Perhaps your earthly body is causing you trouble: your limbs are creaking, your energy is sapped. Your constant visits to the doctor are always inconclusive and frustrating. You can feel your mortality. If that's you, then God wants to inspire you.

The more your body declines, the closer you are to this glorious transformation. If you are in the autumn of your life, and you can feel the weight of winter, then just remember that winter is the gateway to spring.

When the seed is buried in the ground, it is ready for God's glorious transforming power to be unleashed. From frailty to glory. That's the story of our lives. So if sleep is difficult for you, eating food has lost its pleasure, those bodily movements you used to take for granted are becoming strained, then remember, glory is just around the corner. The best is yet to be.

> 'I am resurrection,' Jesus says. By his words, by his miracles, by his resurrection, he brings light and immortality to life through the Gospel. 'I am resurrection'. It isn't just that he raises people, he has risen power in himself. This means that he has to die for us so that he can demonstrate that risen power of God in his own life. You and I need never be afraid of death again, he is saying, 'because I have beaten death' . . . I stood for a moment after we had conducted the funeral service of my father, and in the silence of my mind came the words I had used in the service – 'I am the resurrection and the life.' And then in the silence the words came back to me – 'Jesus has beaten death – do you believe this?'[2] *Liam Goligher*

From Adam's image to Christ's image

A contrast between Adam and Christ dominates the next few verses (44–49). Paul is saying here that we will be transformed from having an Adam kind of body, to having a Christ kind of body. What does he mean by that? Well, it's the difference between having a 'natural' body and a 'spiritual' body. That's the contrast in verse 44: 'if there is a natural body there is also a spiritual body.' To understand this contrast, we need to grasp who we are as human beings. In Genesis 2 we read that Adam was formed from the dust of the earth, a physical, natural creature. And then God breathed into his nostrils the breath of life, and Adam became a living soul.

That's who we are as human beings: children of Adam, the same substance as he was. There is something of the life of God – the breath of God – in us; we have living souls that are eternal. We are different from the animal kingdom.

But we are also from the earth; physical creatures with all the limitations that come with that. We are not like the angels and the spirit world of heaven. From our limited understanding of angels and the spirit world, we realize that they can appear and disappear. They can take on different appearances and so on.

But we are being transformed from Adam's image into Christ's image. When we give our lives to Jesus Christ, we bear his stamp on our souls. We stop being simply physical creatures of the earth, and we start being creatures with the stamp of heaven on us: 'As was the earthly man, so are those who are of the earth; and as is the heavenly man so are those who are of heaven' (verse 48).

We are creatures of a different order now because we are 'in Christ'. And when Christ comes again, our bodies will be transformed from natural bodies to spiritual bodies, just like

Christ; still physical, but of an altogether different order. This is God's breathtaking plan for us.

This means that Christ's holiness and perfection will be ours. All his wisdom and love will be ours. All his beauty and radiance will be ours. We will be immortal and indestructible, and all those words that are beyond our grasp to understand.

What an outrageous plan God has unveiled in Jesus Christ! The gospel is so much more grand and glorious than we often make it out to be. God's plan is for nothing less than cosmic re-creation, for earthly men and women to be transformed from Adam's image to Christ's image.

From defeat to victory

There is a resounding finale to this passage, like the flag-waving on the last night of the Proms. Paul homes in on the fact that as sinful, mortal men and women, we simply aren't ready in our current state for the glory that is to come: 'I declare to you, brothers and sisters, that flesh and blood cannot inherit the kingdom of God, nor does the perishable inherit the imperishable' (1 Corinthians 15:50).

As it stands, our bodies are prone to sin and vulnerable to death. Defeat hangs over our lives from the moment we're born. We try not to think about it. It's not a subject for dinner-time conversation, but as surely as day becomes night, we know that we are going to die.

Twice in this passage Paul mentions the 'sting' of death. The word he uses is the 'sting' of a scorpion or a cobra, reminiscent of the serpent who first tempted Eve to sin in the garden, a painful, debilitating sting that leaves us paralyzed. That's what sin does to us; 'the sting of death is sin' (verse 56).

But for every believer who is placing their hope in the death and resurrection of Jesus Christ, poisonous defeat is transformed into sweet victory. 'Thanks be to God! He gives us the victory through Jesus Christ our Lord' (verse 57).

And now, as believers brimming over with eternal life, we are longing for, crying out for, waiting in electric anticipation for the last great transformation to take place. The finishing line is in sight.

When the clouds are rolled back, and our risen Lord Jesus Christ appears in his glorious resurrected body, riding on the clouds of the air, 'we will all be changed' (verse 52). All of us will be changed, even believers who have been dead for thousands of years.

From dust to glory

Right now believers who have died are just heaps of dust lying in some coffin, ashes at the bottom of some forgotten sea or scattered over some barren hillside. But those dead, decayed, lifeless heaps of dust will be gloriously transformed.

In 'a flash', an instant (verse 52). The word is literally the word for 'atom', a tiny particle that is too small to split. In that 'twinkling of an eye', when the skies are rolled back and Christ appears, we will be transformed: 'For the perishable must clothe itself with the imperishable, and the mortal with immortality' (verse 53), from natural bodies to spiritual bodies.

From the confines of time to the freedom of eternity, from the domain of decay, to the expanse of the new heavens and the new earth. There will be no more tears, no more pain, no more failure, no more shame, no more regret, just glory. Defeat will be swallowed up in victory.

Our inheritance . . . can never perish, spoil or fade . . . the whole universe, according to 2 Peter, burns up with a fierce heat such that even the elements are devoured, but our

inheritance doesn't burn up. It's reserved in heaven for us.
We look for a new heaven and a new earth, the home of
righteousness. It doesn't spoil, it's not defiled . . . There will
be no shred of bitterness, no hate, no arrogance, no greed,
no lust, no envy, no jealousy, no murder, there will be no
harsh tongues – nothing to spoil or corrode our inheritance
. . . this inheritance is kept in heaven for us, and we are kept
for it.[3] *D. A. Carson*

Cosmic renewal

And this promise of renewal is not purely for believers. God
is going to revamp the whole created order. Revelation picks
up an image in Isaiah of God rolling up the heavens 'like a
scroll' (Isaiah 34:4; Revelation 6:14). Peter mentions the
elements being burned up with fire, and the earth and everything in it being laid bare (2 Peter 3:12).

These will be cataclysmic moments in the history of our
universe. This current universe is bound over to decay, as even
physicists will tell you. The second law of thermodynamics is
that all matter, when left to itself, decays.

Our universe has a 'sell-by' date. Our sun, with heat that
travels ninety-three million miles across our solar system to light
up our planet, like every other similar star will die one day. God
planned it that way. The Father has allowed a sense of frustration and decay to be written into this current fallen universe,
to show us how deeply sin impacts on everything it touches.

But God will come finally and swiftly to do away with sin
forever. The climactic renewal of the cosmos, awesome and
fearful as it will be, will have 'grace' written all over it. It will
be an all-out assault, a total destruction of every shadow of
sin from our broken cosmos.

Paul says in Romans 8, in very poetic language, that the creation itself is groaning, awaiting its day of liberation, a liberation from the decay which, like thorns, has been choking it for billions of years.

But incredibly, the creation will not be liberated until we are. The universe is waiting for our final resurrection: 'The creation waits in eager expectation for the children of God to be revealed' (Romans 8:19). The idea behind 'waiting in eager expectation' literally means 'craning its neck'. Like a wide-eyed teenager, lost in a huge crowd, when his favourite band comes on the stage, the whole cosmic order is 'craning its neck', waiting for the moment when our salvation will be complete, and our frail bodies enter into a state of glory. And then, 'The creation itself will be liberated from its bondage to decay and brought into the freedom and glory of the children of God' (Romans 8:21).

The full scope of redemption

I hope you can see the full scope of what was set in motion when the Son of God died and rose from the dead. Three hours of darkness and three days buried in a tomb are only the blink of an eye in the history of the universe.

But the cosmic implications of those brief moments are measureless. Don't limit the full scale of the redemption God has built on the broken body of his Son. So often as Christians we reduce the message of the cross to our personal testimony of how we won our ticket to heaven, and we impoverish our own faith and limit the awe we should feel for the God who saved us for his own glory.

Such thinking is myopic when placed against the magnificent tapestry of God's plans for us in Christ. The death and resurrection of Christ is nothing less than the power that unleashes the death and resurrection of the entire created order.

Christ's cross was, to quote the title of a famous book, 'the day death died', and Christ's resurrection was the moment the power of God obliterated the impact of sin in the whole cosmic order and opened up the way to a future paradise that we could only dream of.

Simply put, Christ's death-burial-resurrection – that salvation event – is the most important thing that has ever, or will ever, happen. You get the feeling that Paul is left breathless at the sheer scale of cosmic redemption, when he says to the Corinthians,

> We declare God's wisdom, a mystery that has been hidden
> and that God destined for our glory before time began.
> None of the rulers of this age understood it, for if they had,
> they would not have crucified the Lord of glory. However as
> it is written,
>
> > 'What no eye has seen,
> >   what no ear has heard,
> > and what no human mind has conceived' –
> >   the things God has prepared for those who
> >   love him.
> (1 Corinthians 2:7–9)

The gospel we believe is a gospel so vast in scope, so limitless in potential, that no one has ever seen anything so marvellous, no ear has ever heard anything so captivating, no mind has ever conceived of anything so glorious. Is that the kind of gospel you have believed, a gospel of cosmic renewal, the meeting of a perfected new heavens, with a liberated new earth?

> The resurrection took but a fraction of a second to accomplish, yet when we pass through the opened and empty tomb we pass into . . . eternity, where we belong, and for which we were created.[4] *Donald G. Barnhouse*

A new vision of glory

I have to confess that often I was left feeling distinctly disgruntled with the visions of heaven that some preachers conveyed to me in my youth. The caricature of sitting on a cloud playing a harp forever or joining in a never-ending worship song made me feel I would rather do anything than go to heaven.

Heaven was seen primarily as a place of rescue. Great, foreboding pictures of hell were created, and heaven was just the alternative place to go if you wanted to avoid getting burned. But I am very thankful that teachers like Tom Wright have re-invigorated my excitement for the glory that awaits:

> Despite what many people think . . . the point of it all is not 'to go to heaven when you die'. The New Testament picks up from the Old the theme that God intends, in the end, to put the whole creation to rights. Earth and heaven are made to overlap with one another, not fitfully, mysteriously and partially as they do at the moment, but completely, gloriously and utterly. 'The earth shall be filled with the glory of the Lord as the waters cover the sea.'
>
> That is the promise which resonates throughout the Bible story . . . The great drama will end, not with 'saved souls' being snatched up into heaven, away from the wicked earth and mortal bodies which have dragged them down

into sin, but with the New Jerusalem coming down from heaven to earth, so that 'the dwelling of God is with humans'.[5]

When heaven meets earth, we will reign with Christ in glorified, but still very physical, bodies and we will know what it means to be perfectly human. As we stand alongside the 'second Adam', we will understand the full joy that even Adam and Eve in their original garden paradise could not enjoy, full, unhindered, unthreatened, liberated, intimate relationship with the God we were made for.

Keep your eye on the prize

Florence Chadwick was a long-distance swimmer, and she became famous in August 1950 for being the first woman to swim the English Channel. But some time later, she made an attempt to swim a twenty-one-mile stretch in California called the Catalina Channel.

After fifteen hours and fifty-five minutes of swimming, with only half a mile to go, and surrounded by boats full of friends and family cheering her on, Florence Chadwick gave up and asked to be taken out of the water.

When she was interviewed later on, no one could believe it. She was a champion swimmer, and she was asked why she had stopped so close to the finishing line. She replied, 'It was the fog.'

She said in her interview, 'If I could only have seen the shore, I know I would have made it.' But because she couldn't see the finishing line, she felt like she was getting nowhere, with aching arms and limbs, so she gave up.

As you run the race of your life for Jesus Christ, with all its ups and downs, temptations and triumphs, successes and sins, power and pain, keep your eyes on the shoreline. Keep your eyes on all the full vista of glory that the resurrection of Jesus has opened up for you.

May the fog roll back, and by the Spirit's grace may you glimpse that glorious transformation you will experience one day when, in an instant, you will be glorious, immortal and holy like the Christ who won this salvation for you.

And you will take your place at Christ's side, at the heart of a renewed cosmos, a place where earth and heaven meet in the most unimaginably beautiful way, and 'God's dwelling place will be among people' (Revelation 21:3).

This glorious hope springs from the death of Christ, yes, but also and especially from his glorious resurrection. Don't sideline the resurrection – the first apostles certainly didn't. The resurrection has enabled the completion of your salvation. It is your hope, your joy, your crown. It's the distant shoreline you are swimming towards. So strain every sinew in your body for King Jesus, 'walk in step with the Spirit', for you will reign with him in glory. That's a promise!

Questions

1. How does the hope of glory make you feel about your present sufferings?
2. Has this chapter changed your understanding of what heaven will be like? Has it increased your excitement? If so, how, and if not, why not?

Passages for further study

Romans 8:18–30; 1 Corinthians 15:20–58; Revelation 21:1–7.

Notes

Note: The main talks of the Keswick Convention have been published in various forms over the years: *The Keswick Week, The Keswick Convention*, and since 1978 as a book with the convention theme as a title. All quotes from these sources indicate the year of the convention.

1. The passion of the cross

1. Preaching Today, <http://www.preachingtoday.com >, under illustrations for June 2004.
2. Sinclair Ferguson, *The Glory of the Gospel*, Keswick 2005 (Authentic), p. 81.
3. 'There is a green hill', Cecil Frances Alexander, 1818–95.
4. Alec Motyer, *The Lord is King*, Keswick 1979 (STL), p. 131.
5. A. St John Thorpe, *The Keswick Week*, 1936, p. 150.

2. The perfect storm

1. Murray J. Harris, 'hyper', in *Dictionary of NT Theology*, ed. Colin Brown (Paternoster, 1986), pp. 1196–1197.
2. D. A. Carson, *Becoming Conversant with the Emerging Church: Understanding A Movement and Its Implications* (Zondervan, 2005).
3. D. A. Carson, *'Deep Impact'*, Keswick 1999 (OM Publishing), p. 253.
4. John R. W. Stott, *The Message of Romans* (IVP, 1994), p. 72.
5. Alistair Begg, *Christ-Centred Renewal*, Keswick 2010 (Authentic), p. 47.
6. Charles Spurgeon, sermon 258, 19 June 1859, <http://www.spurgeon.org/sermons/0258.htm>.
7. Sinclair Ferguson, *The Glory of the Gospel*, Keswick 2005 (Authentic), p. 75.
8. H. Richard Niebuhr, *The Kingdom of God in America* (Harper and Row, 1959 [1936]), p. 193.

9. Ferguson, *The Glory of the Gospel*, p. 79.
10. Chris Byworth, *The Lord is King*, Keswick 1979, p. 117.

3. The headless snake

1. Carolyn Arends, 'Satan's a Goner: A Lesson from a Headless Snake', *Christianity Today*, February 2011.
2. G. B. Duncan, *The Keswick Week*, 1948, p. 98.
3. Eric Metaxas, *Bonhoeffer: Pastor, Martyr, Prophet, Spy* (Nashville, 2010).
4. J. A. Motyer, *The Keswick Week*, 1965, p. 25.
5. Motyer on Hebrews 10:12–13, *Keswick Week*, 1965, p. 24.
6. Motyer, p. 21.
7. J. C. Ryle, *Holiness: Its Nature, Hindrances, Difficulties and Roots* (1877), ch. 1.

4. Justification

1. George Goodman, *The Keswick Convention*, 1936, p. 137.
2. 'Before the throne of God above', Charitie Lees De Chenex, 1841–1923.
3. Alistair Begg, *Christ-Centred Renewal*, Keswick 2010 (Authentic), p. 46.
4. John Bunyan, in Hugh Kerr and John Mulder (eds.), *Famous Conversions* (Eerdmans, 1994), p. 79.
5. John R. W. Stott, *The Keswick Week*, 1965, p. 30.
6. 'When peace like a river', Horatio Gates Spafford, 1828–88.

5. Redemption

1. John R. W. Stott, *The Keswick Week*, 1965, pp. 65–66.
2. 'Reflections', *Christianity Today*, 31 July 2010.
3. George B. Duncan, *The Keswick Week*, 1963, p. 108.
4. Duncan, p. 109.

6. Reconciliation

1. Tim Keller, pastor of Redeemer Presbyterian Church, New York, and author.
2. D. A. Carson, *Deep Impact*, Keswick 1999 (OM Publishing), p. 253.
3. Eric Alexander, *The Keswick Week*, 1973, p. 39.
4. 'And can it be', Charles Wesley, 1707–88.

5. Theo. M. Bamber, *The Keswick Week*, 1948, p. 45.
6. John Piper, sermon 'Much more shall we be saved by his life', 12 December 1999; <http://www.desiringgod.org/resource-library/sermons/much-more-shall-we-be-saved-by-his-life>.
7. Vinay Samuel, quoted from a talk given at Lausanne II, in Spencer Perkins and Chris Price, *More Than Equals: Racial Healing for the Sake of the Gospel* (rev. edn., IVP, 2000), p. 67.
8. Philip Hacking, *The Keswick Week*, 1973, p. 94.
9. Shultz related this to Brian Lamb on the American TV C-Span's 'Booknotes', 27 June 1993; < http://www.booknotes.org/Watch/44051-1/George+Shultz.aspx>.
10. Eric Alexander, *The Keswick Week*, 1973, p. 40.

7. The crossed-out 'I'

1. Helen Roseveare, excerpt from her message 'Motivation for World Mission' at the 1987 IVCF Urbana Missions Convention. See <https://urbana.org/go-and-do/missionary-biographies/courageous-doctor-congo-part-1>.
2. C. S. Lewis, *Mere Christianity* (HarperCollins, 2011 [1952]), ch. 8.
3. Theo. M. Bamber, *The Keswick Week*, 1948, p. 83.
4. Ron Sider, 'A Lot of Lattes', review of *Passing the Plate: Why American Christians Don't Give Away More Money*, in *Christianity Today*, 2010.
5. Eric Alexander, *The Lord is King*, Keswick 1979 (STL), p. 55.
6. E. M. B. Green, *The Keswick Week*, 1964, p. 74.

8. The fellowship of his sufferings

1. Cicero, *Against Verres*, II.66 (Cicero: Political Speeches, Oxford, Oxford University Press, 2006).
2. 'Man of sorrows', Philip Paul Bliss, 1838–76.
3. John R. W. Stott, *The Cross of Christ* (IVP, 1986), pp. 335–336.
4. Donald English, *Real People – Real Faith*, Keswick 1988 (STL), p. 45.
5. I. Howard Marshall, *Acts*, Tyndale NT Commentary (IVP: Leicester, 1980), pp. 123–124.
6. Jonathan Lamb, *Christ-Centred Renewal*, Keswick 2010 (Authentic), p. 130.
7. George Hoffman, *The Cross and the Crown*, Keswick 1992 (OM Publishing), p. 196.

8. Lamb, Keswick 2010.

9. 'When peace like a river', Horatio Gates Spafford, 1828–88.

9. The pilgrim's travel kit

1. 'With harps and with viols', Arthur T. Pierson, 1837–1911.

2. David Jackman, *Real People – Real Faith*, Keswick 1988 (STL), p. 177.

3. Reginald Wallis, *The Keswick Convention*, 1936, p. 128.

4. 'Lord Jesus Christ, we seek thy face', Alexander Stewart, 1870–1950.

5. Francis W. Dixon, *The Keswick Week*, 1962, p. 164.

6. Steve Gaukroger, *The Glory of the Gospel*, Keswick 2005 (Authentic), p. 60.

10. 'If Christ has not been raised . . .'

1. *Portland Monthly Magazine*, January 2010; <http://www.portlandmonthlymag.com/arts-and-entertainment/category/books-and-talks/articles/christopher-hitchens/>; emphasis authors'.

2. D. A. Carson, *Deep Impact*, Keswick 1999 (OM Publishing), p. 27.

3. Theo M. Bamber, 1948, *The Keswick Week*, 1948, p. 46.

4. H. W. Cragg, *The Keswick Week*, 1963, p. 65.

5. Cragg, p. 67.

6. Wolfhart Pannenberg , in a conversation with Ron Sider, *Prism Magazine* (March/April 1997), on <http://www.sermoncentral.com>.

7. A. N. Wilson, *Daily Mail,* 11 April 2009, < http://www.dailymail.co.uk/news/article-1169145/Religion-hatred-Why-longer-cowed-secular-zealots.html>; emphasis authors'.

11. The hope of glory

1. This story comes under 'Illustrations' on preachingtoday.com.

2. Liam Goligher, *Deep Impact*, Keswick 1999 (OM Publishing), p. 217.

3. D. A. Carson, *Deep Impact*, Keswick 1999 (OM Publishing), p. 22.

4. Donald G. Barnhouse, *The Keswick Week*, 1948, p. 206.

5. N. T. Wright, *Simply Christian* (SPCK, 2006) p. 185.

KESWICK MINISTRIES

Keswick Ministries is committed to the deepening of the spiritual life in individuals and church communities through the careful exposition and application of Scripture, seeking to encourage the following:

Lordship of Christ To encourage submission to the Lordship of Christ in personal and corporate living

Life Transformation To encourage a dependency upon the indwelling and fullness of the Holy Spirit for life transformation and effective living

Evangelism and Mission To provoke a strong commitment to the breadth of evangelism and mission in the British Isles and worldwide

Discipleship To stimulate the discipling and training of people of all ages in godliness, service and sacrificial living

Unity To provide a practical demonstration of evangelical unity

Keswick Ministries is committed to achieving its aims by:

- providing Bible based training courses for youth workers and young people (via Root 66) and Bible Weeks for Christians of all backgrounds who want to develop their skills and learn more
- promoting the use of books, DVDs, CDs and downloads so that Keswick's teaching ministry is brought to a wider audience at home and abroad
- producing TV and radio programmes so that superb Bible talks can be broadcast to you at home
- publishing up to date details of Keswick's exciting news and events on our website so that you can access material and purchase Keswick products on-line
- publicising Bible teaching events in the UK and overseas so that Christians of all ages are encouraged to attend 'Keswick' meetings closer to home and grow in their faith
- putting the residential accommodation of the Convention Centre at the disposal of churches, youth groups, Christian organisations and many others, at very reasonable rates, for holidays and outdoor activities in a stunning location

If you'd like more details please look at our website (www.keswickministries.org) or contact the Keswick Ministries office by post, email or telephone as given below.

Keswick Ministries, Convention Centre, Skiddaw Street, Keswick, Cumbria, CA12 4BY

Tel: 017687 80075; Fax 017687 75276; email: info@keswickministries.org